KICK START

A Cosmic Biker Babe's Guide
to Life and Changing the Planet

KICK START

 Carol Setters

CONARI PRESS

First published in 2005 by Conari Press,
an imprint of Red Wheel/Weiser, LLC
York Beach, ME

With offices at:
368 Congress Street
Boston, MA 02210
www.redwheelweiser.com

LIBRARY OF CONGRESS CATALOGING-IN-PUBLICATION DATA
Setters, Carol.
  Kick start : a cosmic biker babe's guide to life and changing the planet /Carol
Setters.
    p. cm.
  Includes bibliographical references and index.
  ISBN 1-57324-214-4 (alk. paper)
  1. Women—Life skills guides. 2. Women—Conduct of life. 3. Self-realization
in women. 4. Conformity. 5. Women motorcyclists. I. Title.
HQ1221.S37 2005
646.7'0082—dc22   2005000654

Book design by Maxine Ressler
Typeset in Minion and Ambrosia Capitals

Printed in Canada
TCP
12   11   10   09   08   07   06   05
   8   7   6   5   4   3   2   1

To Dana and Jim

Contents

Acknowledgments

BEFORE I ACKNOWLEDGE THE PEOPLE WHO HAVE CONTRIBUTED to this book, I should tell you that *The Urantia Book* has been my spiritual guide for thirty years and is the major influence you'll find in these pages. Although the book reflects my own style of seeing things, if you find that perspective intriguing, I invite you to discover its pure essence in *The Urantia Book*.

Red Wheel/Weiser/Conari took a chance on me, and I hope to prove them right. Jan Johnson has a wonderful spirit that she has somehow preserved through what I know is a very tough business. Thanks for knocking me off my chair with that first phone call. My editor, Jill Rogers, is a patient, insightful woman who has taught me a lot about the craft of writing. Thank you for being so tender with my inner author. Many thanks to marketing divas Bonni Hamilton and Emily Logan, who have vigorously and creatively dispelled all those myths about how new authors are ignored when it comes time for promotion. Thanks to Gloria Sturzenacker, who I highly recommend for freelance proofing and editing, and to Susan Osborn, who helped write the Reader's Questions.

I have been blessed with a good support system. My parents trusted me and gave me the confidence to pursue all manner of outrageous dreams and I love them very much. My husband conceptualized the idea of the Biker Planet and helped me run with it, and he is passionate in his devotion to the true love that we share. My teenaged twins miraculously think I'm amusing instead of embarrassing, and everything I've become at this age is just a fraction of what they already are. I live in a community of long-time friends that constantly remind me of what is important in life, and I am grateful to them all.

Most importantly, thanks to God. Regardless of all the things I take issue with such as the need for a third set of teeth, many aspects of the reproductive process, and why life has to be so stinkin' hard, I can't wait to experience more of reality. Thanks for the invitation to play.

Introduction

I USED TO LIVE ON THIS PLANET, BUT I DECIDED TO RELOCATE. I think it was my phone bill that finally pushed me over the edge. It was several years ago, when I was in the middle of paying bills, that the absurdity of it all finally made me snap. There on my phone bill, in the long line of taxes and surcharges, was a deduction of $4.87 for something called the Federal Attrition Reimbursement Charge. What the heck was the Federal Attrition Reimbursement Charge?

I called the phone company to learn the purpose of this particular line item. After being redirected and put on hold for a good hour or so, I was finally connected to a nameless person somewhere in a federal agency who had not yet completed his FIE (Federal Individuality Erasure.) At this point in his training, he was still capable of doing simple, self-directed tasks, and he was nice enough to look up the description of the charge for me. He told me that the Federal Attrition Reimbursement Charge has something to do with reimbursing the federal government for paying monies to families who lost loved ones in the military during the War of 1812. There was really nothing I could do but pay it or have my phone service disconnected. He was polite, but firm.

That did it. I couldn't help but believe that somewhere out in the universe, life had to make more sense. The more I thought about it, the more attractive it sounded to live my life on another world, so I packed my bags and left for a while. I had a lot of interesting experiences, but hard as I tried, I just never quite fit in. It took me a while to find a good interpreter, and I later learned that I had been the brunt of a lot of "Earth jokes." One inter-galactic favorite starts with the question "How many Earthlings does it take to get a spacecraft up to warp speed?" I don't remember the exact punch line, but it has something to do with a hamster wheel. It got old. After a while, I was ready to come home and admit my citizenship on one of the wackier planets in the Milky Way.

Earth really is different from the other worlds I visited. *Different* doesn't adequately describe the contrast. The truth of the matter is: Life on our planet is stranger than science fiction. Just being transported to a normal world would make you think you had died and gone to heaven. Other planetary races in this part of the galaxy see us as a fascinating experiment in mortal evolution. They're all taking bets on whether we'll manage to survive another century.

Of course, for anyone with half a brain, the idea that something went awry here is hardly news. That some people are dying from obesity while others are starving to death, or that we have thousands of organizations trying to eradicate disease while the tobacco industry launches a campaign targeted at young people, or that executives from large corporations make off with millions of dollars that belong to their employees and they never get held accountable, are just a few examples of the insanity that runs amuck here.

The other planets I visited didn't have these glaring dichotomies, and I think I know why. One of the biggest differences between the culture on Earth and the cultures on other planets is that the more progressive worlds encourage their citizens to develop their unique skills and make a difference. Imagine that. They actually value the genius of their people in improving their global condition. We think of it a little differently here. On Earth, we believe that the bulge in the middle of the bell curve is a beautiful thing. It makes life easier, mostly for bureaucracies and marketing firms.

That one difference seems to be the key to the larger difference between evolving as a species and, well, whatever it is we're doing instead. I saw how it's supposed to work firsthand on other planets, and it was very inspiring. I figured as long as I was coming back here to live, I might as well try to share some of the insights I gained and become an ambassador of a better way. It's not such a far-fetched idea. If we could think a little more for ourselves and exercise a little more mental stamina to come up with some real inspiration, we could have better lives than we do. As it is, we're mindlessly working toward goals that really don't matter. We need to get rid of a lot of things on this planet, but from what I learned out in the universe, one of the most critical problems we could eradicate is our habit of conformity.

In keeping with the tradition of every yahoo who thinks they have something important to say, I decided to write a book. I would do my best to encourage people to become more authentic. But I knew that we're so overloaded with all manner of information that I'd have to make my message as vivid and compelling as possible. (I learned this from overloading myself with all manner of information from books written by marketing gurus.) So I set out to find an inspiring symbol to personify my message, someone who captures the rugged determination of an individualist. The person I would choose couldn't be your normal, garden-variety symbol—because as I said, there's nothing normal about any of us. We can't aspire to the ideal of a perfect person if we know such a person has a slim chance of ever appearing on this planet.

Earthlings are strange, with all manner of quirks. So the symbol for this new concept of individuality would have to be someone who would personify courage, loyalty, determination and other noble attributes that make us worthy to continue as a species. But the person would have to be someone who also honestly represents what we really are. The icon I'd choose would have to be a courageous and slightly askew individualist. A person unafraid to take on the dangers of being out there in the world with nothing but her will to survive and the ability to endure the ridicule of being different.

Sometimes inspiration comes to us in strange ways. I was out for a motorcycle ride with my husband one day (I ride my own, thank you), and while we were riding, the shifter rod on his motorcycle decided that now would be a good time to fall off. It started flopping around wildly. The shifter rod is what you use for shifting gears, and it's virtually impossible to ride a motorcycle without one, but we were nowhere near home or a repair shop.

My husband did what any intelligent person would do—he pulled out the duct tape. He keeps a big roll of it in his emergency kit, and he rigged a rather ingenious temporary solution to get going again. The motorcycle could do nothing more than limp along in second gear, but at least he made it home.

Upon reflection, I realized we had experienced a good metaphor for life on Earth: Just when you're finally at a comfortable speed and you're making progress in life, something falls off. The way we fix the problem is rarely the ideal solution we would choose in ideal circumstances. We end up having trouble regaining enough speed to accomplish anything we originally set out to do, but we generally make it back home. A fitting symbol for the people and the planet? Yeah. A Biker will do just fine. Henceforth, I shall refer to Planet Earth as the Biker Planet.

If I had to choose between being associated with the image of a Soccer Mom and that of a Biker, I guarantee you I'd choose the Biker. The Biker character represents some of the most endearing qualities people exhibit on this world, namely the courage and mental stamina it requires to escape mind-numbing conformity and standardization. Bikers follow their hearts, and they're unafraid to go wherever the road leads them. They also represent something inside of us that we're a little afraid of: the possibility that if we acted like ourselves, we wouldn't fit in. If we wore our true nature on the outside, people would stare.

But women who embody these Biker qualities are all around us, and they follow what they believe is the right thing to do, regardless of how different they appear from everyone else. The type of woman who quits her high-paying corporate job to pursue her art doesn't care that her lifestyle won't reflect the trappings of material success anymore. And the woman who digs up her thirsty green lawn and lets her yard return to its natural state is happy to put up with disapproving looks from neighbors. She cares more about the consequences of wasting massive quantities of water than she does about fitting in.

But there are other reasons the Biker is a good representative of the people of this planet. Whether or not you like the association with some of society's more fringe elements, you have to admit that Earthlings in general share with the Biker culture a fascination for power and speed. Loud motors, especially on fast vehicles, excite something inside of us. It shows up in kids early on—many babies learn to make motor noises long before they can talk. Kids run or twirl as fast as they can until they fall down from vertigo or exhaustion. It's obvious that people on this planet like to go, and go fast.

In addition to the fact that motorcycles are powerful, noisy machines, they give us reality at high speed—sort of like channel-surfing the world. In the same way the bicycle revolutionized personal mobility, motorcycles revolutionized the speed of what we can experience in the great outdoors. In a dizzying, fabulous cacophony of stimulus, motorcycling is a traveling reality feast.

Have you ever ridden a motorcycle on a Sunday afternoon when the sun is shining and the air is warm? In the spring you can smell the lilacs, and in the summer you can smell hamburgers being grilled in backyards. You feel the change in temperature and humidity between the city and the country. All of reality is whirled into a stunning vignette of life while moving along the surface of the planet on a rumbling, powerful engine and two wheels, with nothing else between you and the road. The motorcycle is the twenty-first century's instrument for experience. In my opinion, which I respect.

If you're not a Biker and you don't know any, you may still harbor a Hollywood-esque idea of who Bikers are. Back in the 1960s and '70s, a string of badly written movies portrayed all

Bikers as marauding bands of hoodlums who would ride into town and start trouble with the locals. They were favorite villains for a lot of B-rated plots. But Bikers were never limited to one social stratum.

In reality, every race, income bracket and occupation is present in the Biker Culture, and more people are joining every day. While old-time motorcyclists loathe the mainstreaming of their cult, the Biker image no longer represents just a small contingent of outlaws and tough guys anymore. Instead of being told to leave, the Biker in the leather jacket is often considered the trendiest person in the place.

Riding a motorcycle has become increasingly popular because it is unlike anything else you can do to get from one place to another. It firmly places the rider in a conscious relationship with the world at a time when people are craving something outside of their bland, cushy, overstimulated-in-a-voyeuristic-kind-of-way lives. It's hard to explain, but to ride a motorcycle is to Be Here Now.

It was cash that finally made the motorcycle industry begrudgingly acknowledge the fact that women were not going to remain the Bitches on the Back forever. In recent years, motorcycle manufacturers have realized that women are purchasing motorcycles in ever-growing numbers, so more choices for women are being designed these days. In addition to the fact that women are gaining increasing social liberty to express themselves, more and more sisters are enjoying the ride from the front.

An interesting take on how a woman Biker defines herself was once posted online at a Biker website:

[1] Biker Chick, n. A girl, woman, et cetera who rides motorcycles of any brand or origin. She is not afraid to take control of her destiny, or to take risks. She is gifted with a strong desire for adventure and fun, and finds both atop a bike. Biker Chicks are not the property of anyone but themselves, and will not be intimidated by social mandates of what girls/ladies/women should and should not do.

As a symbol, the Biker may be even more compelling for women than for men. Women are awakening to the fact that their power comes from authenticity, not from conformity. We are coming to the realization that the exquisite strength inherent in our gender must be expressed more openly if we are going to participate in saving this planet from its current state of chaos.

Women in the Western world are now in their third century of a full-on crusade for the right to self-determine what and who we can be. Many of us are working hard to pass and protect policies and laws that support human rights in America and around the globe, but we still have our biggest challenge before us. More women must own, in their heart of hearts, the belief that their opinions and ideas matter, and that this self-determination deserves to be supported in both society and their own lives. It is invigorating to join others and demonstrate in support of women's rights, but then we have to come home and live it.

The most decisive factor in making us who we are emerges from the beliefs we carry about our right to act on our own convictions. Each one of us is a unique daughter of God, with a distinctive combination of strengths and personality traits that will never be duplicated in any other human being. Our life experiences contribute to make each of us a singular, distinctive woman. And that's exactly who we should strive to be—because until we develop our individual brilliance, we can't expect the world to change much.

Perhaps *Kick Start* will move you to let that brilliance shine. I've included stories here that you'll recognize from your own world—lessons I've learned from hard experiences and from reading about other women's challenges through my Cosmic Biker website, www.*cosmicbiker.com*. Some of these issues may not represent where you are in your life right now, but hopefully some of them will challenge you and help you grow.

I've included exercises to help you think out loud, as it were, about the assumptions you may be carrying to help you replace tired habits with supportive ones. I hope you'll be compelled to examine your personal perspective and set of values to make the particular road you travel even more valuable to your life and the people whose lives you touch.

You may consider getting together with other women to form a reader's group to support each other as you consider these issues. To this end, I have included discussion questions in an appendix at the back of this book that explore the ideas in the chapters. I've also offered suggestions about how to develop such a group.

No matter how you do it, I invite you to plunge headlong and passionately into uncharted territory. Muster the courage to develop your individual gifts and strengths as the fabulous woman you truly are. Make a continuous effort to discover what's important to your heart and then be unswervingly loyal to those ideals.

We are being called to a new era, Sisters. It is the Era of the SheBiker.

The SheBiker

My grandmother was one of the few college-educated women of her generation. She was a brilliant woman, but not smart enough to marry the right guy. As it turns out, she married a cad. In what must have been a tough decision, she and her three children ended up moving back in with her mother. To support her family during hard times, she was able to secure a job sewing buttons on shirts in a factory, where she collected fifteen cents for each shirt she completed. Fifteen cents with a college degree.

She also filed for divorce, which she knew would make her a permanent outcast from society. Never mind that her husband continually gambled away all their money and left her and the children in abject poverty, or that he drank and disappeared for days. She would be the one who would carry the mark of distinction as a "divorcée."

My mother was the youngest of her three children. "One day," my mother told me, "when I was about five years old, my father showed up at the house during the day while my mother was working. He told the three of us that we were going for a ride, and we walked down the dusty road to the highway and hitched a ride on a flatbed truck. We didn't know where we were going, but he was our father, so we didn't question him. We rode and rode for hours. My mother came home after a hard day to an empty house and three missing children."

My mother doesn't remember much about the next few days except that they stayed in a seedy hotel, ate animal crackers, and waited for their father to return from wherever it was he went every morning. Unbeknownst to them, he was arranging their sale as a way to exact revenge on his wife for leaving him. To his credit, he did not attempt to place them in the darker opportunities that were most likely available. He actually spent some effort trying to find them a decent home.

My grandfather was unable to sell the two older children, but my mother was only five and absolutely adorable. He found a couple whose own young daughter had recently died, and he conned them into believing that his wife had died and he was unable to care for his daughter any longer. "I saw my father one more time after he dropped me off," my mother said. "He came back, evidently to collect some money, and I remember standing outside when he left, watching his car until it disappeared out of sight."

My grandfather put the two older children on the bus and sent them back home. Wasn't that nice of him. When the bus let them out at their hometown, they ran down the dusty road, burst in the door of the house, and embraced my startled grandmother. They told her they didn't know where their sister was and they knew they would never see her again.

Every weekend, my grandmother's two brothers would pick her up in the car one of them owned, and the three of them systematically drove to all the orphanages and children's homes in the region, hoping to find her five-year-old daughter.

Meanwhile, my mother was trying to adjust to her new life. "Even at that age, I knew the rest of the family didn't approve of me," my mother said. "I felt awkward and out of place." She started school, but she couldn't concentrate. She developed a stutter, which she struggles with to this day. She couldn't understand why no one would listen to her when she told them her mother hadn't died.

Every Sunday, my mother's nanny would take my mother with her as she visited her own family on her day off. My mother would tell them her mother was still alive, but of course everyone just assumed that such a small child was unable to fathom the death of her mother, and they never followed up on her story. Until the nanny was fired.

The nanny addressed a postcard to "Mrs. Chapman, Mulvane Kansas" and wrote down the whereabouts of my mother. Back then, such a postcard actually had a chance of arriving at its destination. I guess the nanny felt she owed it to my mother to make one effort to see if the little girl knew what she was talking about. Or perhaps everyone knew it all along and never talked about it. In a defining stroke of luck, my grandmother got the postcard in the mail. My mother remembers being out on the driveway skipping rope when the Highway Patrol car pulled up and my grandmother burst from the car.

"When we arrived back home, my mother took the clothes I was wearing, washed them, and sent them back to the couple in Oklahoma," my mother told me. Later on that year, my young mother was put on the witness stand in the courtroom to tell the story of what had happened, and the judge in the divorce case actually granted my grandmother her requested divorce. Judges at that time determined such life-changing civil decisions as if they somehow had the Solomon-like wisdom to do that sort of thing. Women weren't considered competent to make those decisions for themselves. And my grandfather was never prosecuted for any of his actions.

I remember my grandmother in her older years as a diminutive, sharp individual. She crafted a career for herself in the health care industry, where she was well respected. She fell in love with a terminally ill gentleman she met at the hospital, and they married. He died shortly thereafter. But at least she knew true love in her lifetime, and for that, I am grateful.

I don't know if I could have withstood all the insults my grandmother endured. To be so intelligent and so capable and to have every aspect of society pushing her down must have been maddening at times. But she still created a successful life for herself. Unlike other women who are more fortunate in the way things turn out in their lives, women like my grandmother have a very definite way of seeing things, forged from the difficulties they experience. Difficulties often compel us to reach so deep in ourselves for strength that we move beyond the identity we wear on the outside, beyond the face we put on for the public, for our families and even for the mirror, and we find something more. In that authenticity, we find power. On this planet, it's a power that is not supported in society. Because it is at odds with how the world often wants to treat us, it gives us a certain hard edge in our resolve. We know what we are capable of, and we cannot go back to accepting the limitations that the world would impose on us. We become SheBikers. My grandmother would have looked pretty awesome in a leather jacket.

When women go through the kind of experience my grandmother went through, they become connected to a vast reservoir of strength and inspiration that comes from something overwhelmingly enormous—a deep, deep vein of aliveness that has no beginning and no end. This is the divine connection that gives us our power. And if a woman can take that connection into her everyday existence, she realizes that external approval and social acceptance are paltry echoes of the validation she receives from the Source.

Some women revel in their authenticity. Most of us don't trust it. By the time you finish reading this book, you will never be able to go back to doubting that who you are is exactly good enough.

Two movements are occurring at the same time in the collective female realization of strength. One is the cultural change that allows our daughters and our sons to readily accept the true nature of a female. The other is the Coming-of-Strength of baby boomer women. While I have evolved in this long, painful awakening, I have carefully cultivated important perceptions in my teenage daughter. Her environment, for the most part, supports those perceptions. But for me, it required years of peeling away layers of conformity and negative messages. No one told me back in grade school that we'd end up here, and if you had described to me then what we've become today, it would have sounded stranger than fiction.

In the mid-twentieth century, when the boomers were growing up, few women rode their own motorcycles, fewer moms campaigned for abortion rights, and my mother never told me to keep quiet while she meditated.

Back then, the world was a different place. And I thought my future would be different from the way it turned out. I believed what I saw on TV and thought my life would turn out like the characters I saw perform for canned laughter between commercials. I thought my teenage years would be fun and crazy, just like Gidget's life. I thought I'd get married and live like Samantha on the sitcom Bewitched, but without the magic powers. My version of Darrin would come home every evening from his advertising job, we'd have cocktails before dinner, and life would be just peachy.

One day when I was in the fifth grade, the health room nurse called all the girls out of class for a "little talk" and handed out booklets printed and distributed by a company that wanted to sell us sanitary napkins in the very near future. Holding the booklet in my freckled hands, I was fixated on the cover. It had a drawing of a beautiful white-bread young girl in pigtails and rolled-up jeans, primping in front of a curtained vanity table. She was smiling at herself in the mirror, and the image looking back wore a pink, frilly dress with bows in her shiny, wavy hair. Written across the booklet's cover in the heavy script font everybody used back then were the words "You're a Young Lady Now!"

I coveted the Young Lady's life. She looked so pretty in that pink dress, and you could just *tell* she was happy by her confident smile. I couldn't *wait* to start my period and become a Young Lady, too!

Oh, *yeah*! Womanhood! Back then, we had cute little flowered cloth bags that held sanitary napkins and tampons so we didn't have to "advertise," for God's sake, that we were, well, you know, at that time of the month. There was nothing more mortifying than some indication that you were on your period. Horrors. A stain for all to see.

But the truth is, the greatest strength I have as a female seems to be rooted in a menstrual period. As tough as guys are, they've never experienced the pain of abdominal cramps month after month after month after year after year. It gives women a special ability to put up with discomfort and keep moving forward, which can be a useful strength, considering how uncomfortable life on the Biker Planet can be.

And while enduring discomfort can be a strength, the biggest challenge a woman has in that endurance is to not get caught up playing the martyr. Long-suffering may be an attribute, but not in and of itself. There's nothing virtuous about suffering if it doesn't further positive goals.

It's appalling how many times women are rewarded on this planet for being martyrs. When a man in the public eye cheats on his wife, her face appears on the cover of magazines and everyone indirectly lauds her ability to endure such humiliation. Take that same woman and highlight her efforts toward empowering herself, and there will be as many people who not-so-indirectly criticize her for being uppity.

Don't be afraid of your strength. If you use it only for pain medication, it ends up distorting your personality. You get that weird self-righteous martyr thing going where you start having long conversations in your head about how good you are to put up with such crap. We don't need long-suffering if it can be avoided. Get out there and train the world to accept the fact that you're strong and you're staying that way. Don't back off just because it makes others uncomfortable.

Social pressures hold us down, but they aren't all we battle against. We struggle, not only against the status quo, but against our own inner voices. If you're like me, you were probably trained as a little girl to be "nice." It can be the kiss of death for your potential as a person. You won't hear people telling boys they need to be "nice," but girls are expected to give it top priority.

And this expectation continues beyond childhood. Women care a great deal about what people think, so as not to get the disturbing message that those around us are uncomfortable with who we are. Men would be considered strange if they were so preoccupied about what other people think.

Push beyond that early training. Do what you need to do to be true to your goals for personal development and for your service to the planet. When you start to come up against barriers in other people, realize it's not personal, you're just knocking them out of their complacency. Most people still want women to act in a very narrowly defined way. When you act differently, people are forced off automatic and have to be in the moment, and that takes effort.

Any time you make people exert effort, you're going to come up against resistance. Don't bother wasting your own energy by reacting to their resistance. If your primary goal is to change the way other people think, then by all means, go ahead and take the time to argue with them. But if that isn't your goal, then get on with it, no matter what "their" opinions are. If your goals are progressive and true, have faith the Great Unwashed will follow. Eventually.

So how does a SheBiker exhibit her strength? We're all aware of the strange mutant women who dressed and acted like men back in the last half of the twentieth century in order to make it in the business world. They felt they had to be that way, and I don't know, maybe they did. But things are not as limiting now. It may not be a finished model yet, but opportunities to present ourselves as our Real Selves are more prevalent today. They're an important ongoing training program for the planet. We need to make no bones about the fact that we're not strong like a man, we're strong like a woman, and we're powerful, sexy, compassionate and brilliant. In other words, we're SheBikers.

As we're working to accurately reflect an authentic expression of who we are, we should also remember the goal of supporting strength in all women of our native sphere, the Biker Planet. We have our own spiritual and intellectual evolution to attend to, but we also have a duty to help the species evolve. The sooner women—and men—feel comfortable actualizing who they really are instead of what they think they should be, the sooner we'll have a beautiful, peaceful place to live.

As it is now, many of us don't quite know how to be authentic and powerful. Yet. Sometimes a woman hasn't replaced the nice part she's discarded with anything else, and you end up with a Bitch. But maybe she isn't. Don't be too quick to judge the sisters who are breaking new ground. They're busy doing things other than making sure they're likable. For many of us, that finely tuned ability to make sure we're likable is a skill that holds us back.

Women are experts at reading a situation quickly and thoroughly, and we have used that ability to manipulate the hell out of men over the eons. It was a good talent to have for women when physical strength ruled the day. But it's one of those early survival tools that has outlived its usefulness in a lot of situations.

The problem is not the assessment tool in our mind. It's the parasite that lives next to the assessment tool—the Approval Whore. In all my conversations with women, this nasty addiction appears to be one of the most difficult demons to exorcise. It's so deep that it almost defies our ability to move beyond it. Until every woman feels the power to develop her true self and renounce her dependence on being shaped and guided by others, we won't have a healthy human race. Yes, we are a family and we listen to the wisdom of others. But that does not replace personal conviction.

Perhaps society has trained us to believe we shouldn't trust what we think and feel, or perhaps we naturally lack confidence. Whatever the reason, with our ill-defined focus and free-form anxiety, some women have turned to strange leaders for guidance: our country's retailers. Massive retail corporations have invested billions of dollars into advertising campaigns to train us to behave the way they'd like us to behave.

Want to know who you're supposed to be? Just watch any commercial. The retailer's ideal woman has no money problems. Her interests revolve around a trendy, immaculate home and the sales events at her favorite department store—when she's not running a board meeting in a designer business suit. She's thin and Victoria's Secret gorgeous, her life can be transformed with the right car or stovetop meal, and her kids never talk back to her. Her husband is a befuzzled oaf she happily guides through difficulties, and all of her problems are solved in fifteen to thirty seconds through the introduction of a new product.

Yes, that's an overgeneralization, yet many, many women unconsciously measure themselves against this ridiculous caricature of a human female. And while the Madison Avenue effort to influence us has been here for a long time, it is more pervasive than ever before.

Most of us are following these subtle messages with no idea whatsoever why we are supposed to do or think or act in those ways. Many of the trends we so painstakingly follow *have* no reason to them except to make us better consumers. We latch on to other trends because we think being like everyone else is a good thing. If that's true, why aren't we happier?

It's essential to rebel against conformity as it exists today, because conformity as it exists today sucks. If there were something decent about most of the status quo that helped us become better people, then it would be worth the effort to become standardized. But that's not how humans are. Our beauty is in our uniqueness, not in our efforts to mold ourselves into a static model of something we're not.

Sometimes we struggle with things that make no sense because we've been told they'll make us acceptable. Listen to your gut. God is the maker of all reality; truth isn't some addition to life that is at odds with reasonableness. Truth can be lived in any situation. If you believe what you're feeling is true, and it is different than what you are being asked to do, then find another way.

Not only can truth be lived in any condition, truth adds value to your self-worth by making you more real. Life doesn't necessarily get easier, but when you consistently act upon what you believe in, and you don't get tossed about from trend to trend, life becomes much more sane.

As we search for truth and struggle to live it, we will undoubtedly make mistakes. And if we make mistakes, will we say, "I'm not smart enough to do this"?

Not if we stop seeing mistakes as failures. Mistakes are genuine progress toward success. You've just figured out one more way that it can't be done. You've just tweaked your direction so you're more in line with the truth. Perfection can't be achieved in a lifetime on this planet, but it is still the finest goal. Have you ever seen anyone here who was perfect? Of course not, so don't be too hard on yourself.

Life is about growth. You've most likely learned more through your mistakes than you have through your successes. If you begin seeing mistakes as valuable learning tools, you'll be less likely to resort to choosing safe decisions. Safe decisions are good, but growth decisions are better. And besides, sometimes our inability to do something is not completely our fault. This is one crazy world. Lots of things don't work here. Even when it is our fault when mistakes occur, it's okay to show our imperfections.

We have millions and millions of years to become perfect and to satisfy all of our longings. Our accomplishments don't all have to be safely tucked away into our Superwoman portfolio before we leave the planet.

There are so many more important goals than driving a new SUV or having designer thighs. It's disturbing to meet women who are merely aspiring to the status quo. What woman in her right mind would want to become the reigning Miss Planet Earth? We've got exciting new paths to blaze, Sisters, and God has already given us the spirit and intelligence to make it happen.

SheBikers are at the threshold of the most exciting epoch of our gender's history. Women are slowly emerging from centuries of domination by cultural tradition. As this planet's nations become more amalgamated through the free exchange of information and ease of travel, we have a brand new opportunity to join hands with women everywhere and take advantage of the decidedly feminine power of cooperation. It's already happening all over the world, and it is only a matter of personal willingness to join in this exciting adventure. We need to support one another as we exercise the faith to let go of our dependence on approval and guidance from outside sources, and chart our course, instead, by the convictions within us.

The challenge for most of us is that we've been so busy taking care of absolutely everyone but ourselves that we no longer know what our convictions are. I was already at that point by the time I was sixteen. People would ask me, "What do you want to do with your life?" I thought it was a trick question. What did I want to do? What did it matter? What do *you* want me to do?

But that place of inner conviction was building and growing inside me, despite my inability to consciously relate to it. I was forming opinions on what I believed in, what mattered to me, and what I loved. I just didn't act on any of it.

When you spend years and years contorting yourself into something that isn't really you, you develop some pretty bizarre behaviors, not to mention make some pretty funny choices. Funny may be the wrong word . . .

Self-Imposed Roadblocks

My perfect fantasy: I'm at home one day and I hear a knock at my door. Upon opening the door, I find the Queen SheBiker standing there with her magic wand. In my mind, the Queen looks a little like Glenda the Good Witch from *The Wizard of Oz*, only dressed in black leather. The big hair still works.

The Queen gives me a sympathetic smile. She waves her magic wand over me a few times and—*presto!* Life is extraordinary and easy all in one fell swoop.

The first order of business is how the Queen solves all my financial problems. Suddenly I have a billfold so stuffed with money I can barely close it. More money instantly appears when I peel off a few bucks to buy groceries or put gas in my motorcycle tank.

The Queen would make my life easier, too. My children would actually do what they were told. Solutions to life's problems would fall in my lap, and I would never again have to phone someone ten times before I finally got them to take my call. Life would be on the fast track.

Then I could take the risk of letting my real self live on the outside. If I weren't indentured to all these financial institutions, and my children's insane schedule, and all the other Duty Vortexes that drain me dry, I could change my life and change the world.

I suppose it's common to feel trapped in a pedestrian existence. How are we supposed to be outrageous women when our lives are filled with mundane tasks like typing away on keyboards all day, doing laundry, or arguing with the phone company? Other than a few lucky adventurers, who among us gets a chance to lead a life that makes a difference?

Well, Sisters, it's time to figure out how it's done. It isn't a matter of something happening *to* us—like everything else, we've got to *make* it happen. We can create a real change that allows us to develop the genuine woman inside who has so much more to offer and experience. That's when the adventure begins.

To live the kind of life that's satisfying and gives us the chance to do exceptional things, it is essential to rise to the challenge of *becoming* an exceptional person. That exceptional person is already present in each one of us, but she's more than likely covered up with layers of conformity.

Most of us are unconscious conformists, gradually agreeing to an agenda for our lives that is set by someone and everyone else. Practically everything we do is narrowly focused into a grouping of lifestyle choices and activities that, when viewed in their entirety over a lifetime, make you want to retch for having settled for such piffle. But it's our own doing. We don't pay enough attention to what's going on, and slowly but surely, we get stuck in ruts in which we believe we're compelled to stay.

There's a way out, and the change begins with our perspective. We already have what it takes to change—God has given each one of us the amazing gifts of creativity and free will. But to release those gifts and allow them to work their magic in our lives, we have to spend some mental energy. We have to think about what that beautiful woman inside of us stands for, what we want for the world, and whether or not we want it badly enough to face our shortcomings and move beyond them.

Most of us grew up in an environment where we were encouraged to conform to particular social standards. People are rewarded for being like everyone else. But we know that we're not all alike. Pretending we are is a contorting, perverting, unrealistic way to live. Insincerity is at the root of unhappiness.

We cannot actualize our dreams if we are not living a real life. Our power comes from being genuine and from a wholehearted commitment to the vision that comes from that authenticity. It's impossible to realize your own dreams at the same time you're trying to be someone you're not.

If we are going to get on with the business of becoming She-Bikers, women who are unafraid to live our own destinies on the tough Biker Planet, we have to take a hard look at where we are now. Most of us struggle with similar issues, because most of our struggles are about trying to make ourselves fit into the same mold.

Conformity is society's way of helping people do as little thinking as possible. When people are around someone who is different from them, it requires them to pay attention. In other words, it requires effort to assimilate the impression of another person if we don't have particular visual cues, and humans aren't big on effort. So they create shortcuts, and one of them is appearance.

Our belief that we must conform to a certain standard of physical appearance is one of the worst barriers we experience in our efforts to become real. Many women are slaves to how they think they should look, which is almost always something different than how they look naturally. They rely on artificiality to bring them the attention they crave, and to create an acceptable persona.

Women who spend a lot of time around each other, whether it's through business, community interests, or social groupings, tend to have their own little dress code. Some women have big hair, while others have it shortly cropped. Some women wear preppy navy, while others require pastels. Whatever the particulars, women spend an inordinate amount of time in front of the mirror, beating their hair into submission and applying the appropriate amount of makeup to look the way the other women in their social circle look.

I was fortunate. The one man I wanted to be beautiful for saved me. My husband told me shortly after we fell in love that he couldn't see my beautiful eyes because of all of that "black stuff"

I had on my lashes. I nearly dropped my mascara wand. Wow, someone likes the way I look naturally? What planet is this person from?

Women manipulate their looks like a science. Their hair, their nails, their body parts. I used to have fake nails and had to return to the salon to get them redone every two weeks. I sat there one day holding hands with my middle-aged nail technician as she filed away at the perfectly curved extensions of acrylic I had glued to my fingers and thought, What am I *doing*? These are just finger-nails, for God's sake! I peeled them off later and never went back.

The confusion we all seem to suffer from regarding whether we're valuable can be traced back to our parents and blamed solely on them. (Just kidding, Mom and Dad!) No, really, at some point we need to recognize that as adults, we should admit to our feelings of unworthiness, no matter where they come from, and correct those feelings.

What is valuable in a human being? How can we be sure our efforts to feel valuable will be successful? Where does the essence of true worthiness reside in a human life?

The answer, like most other valuable realizations, requires a leap of faith. If you've been relying on an artificial smoke screen, which usually fools you more than it does others, "coming out" can be a frightening thing to consider. Some of us don't even know what it means to be real. But reality is no joke. You've got to develop the true essence of who you are and achieve some internal momentum if you want your soul to continue beyond the expiration date of your body.

People who are genuine develop their own talents and per-sonalities, often rising to the top of our society by becoming lead-ers or innovators. Take, for instance, Lisa Fernandez, the Olympic Gold Medalist who played on the U.S. softball team or Madeleine Albright, the former Secretary of State. Neither of these women would have made significant contributions to their respective spheres of influence without making the day-to-day decisions that led them down their unique paths in life. There are many more examples, most of whom are never known outside their own communities. They are often the most satisfied and effective people on the planet, because they are true to the realness of who they are.

One of the most powerful qualities of real individuals is that they seem to care very little about what other people think. People who are genuine slowly but surely follow their heart and develop a lifestyle and life purpose that intensifies as they grow older.

Samantha Power, the award-winning Pulitzer Prize author, has followed a life purpose that sprang from her years of journalism in Bosnia, where she witnessed firsthand the horrors of genocide. America's apathy toward the crimes in Bosnia, along with its inaction toward nearly every act of genocide in the last century, was instrumental in developing her life purpose. She writes about America's dysfunction in international policies for an American public that finds her revelations disquieting. She doesn't care. She insists that we look at a side of our national identity that hardly matches how we prefer to see ourselves, regardless of the unpopularity of her viewpoint, because she knows that it's real.

Like Samantha, women who've spent time being true to themselves invariably dedicate their lives to a cause greater than themselves. They know who they are, and they recognize they are part of a greater whole. Actively serving a greater purpose creates a bigger person than simply serving the tyrannical trio of Me, Myself and I.

How do you become such a richly real individual? One thing that doesn't work is keeping a running tab on what's popular right now and changing accordingly. That's only an echo of the real thing in someone else.

If you dedicate yourself to discovering the values that are eternally real, you will slowly evolve a unique viewpoint of what is important in life. However, some people stop there and just talk about it, without ever showing evidence that they've actually put those discoveries to work in their lives. A perfect example is a member in a religious movement who talks and talks about truth and love but still condemns people who don't think exactly the way he or she does. Such people have only an intellectual perception of what is valuable. It takes courage to go one more step and let the vision flow through you into your life.

Once you've begun to discern what makes a person real, dedicate yourself to waking up. Whether you use the exercises later in this book or develop your own process for defining the things you stand for, you must examine every decision you make in terms of whether it takes you closer to your core identity or further away. When your decisions are consistently focused on what you stand for and what you believe in, you will become more real and your life will acquire a certain flow. Not that things are easier. But dedicating yourself to recognizing what is important, and then mobilizing the self-discipline to make decisions and choose thoughts that incorporate those values in your life, will give you more self-respect. Absolutely. And you will begin to clearly see how to use your brilliance to make a difference in the world.

Becoming more real doesn't mean you are any less elegant, gracious or fabulous. It means you possess those traits in a genuine way. Instead of pretending to be beautiful according to some arbitrary standard, you develop the things about yourself that are truly beautiful. There's a power in authenticity that can't be expressed when you're only projecting a shadow of the real thing.

God doesn't make losers. We craft those masks ourselves. Dedicating yourself to becoming who you were intended to be is the surest path to becoming extraordinary, and to leading an extraordinary life.

Sorting through the things that are real, and the things that are there only for show, is not something most people are working on. As a matter of fact, the whole world seems to be hopelessly devoted to proving just how much they look like everyone else, not only in physical appearance, but in lifestyle as well.

My husband occasionally watches television shows that feature people who remodel their homes. He recently saw a show in which a couple had remodeled the kitchen in their 6,000-square-foot house to include restaurant-style appliances and enough room in the kitchen for guests to mingle and have "fun" (spoken with a crinkle in one's nose) while the couple cooked impressive and entertaining meals. Every aspect of their discussion with the show's host about their own home was focused on how it would impress others. They never once mentioned how their house and its design made them feel personally. Terry told me he couldn't help but imagine how cavernous the place was when they weren't entertaining. The thought of the two of them echoing around in their enormous kitchen while making the morning coffee made them seem silly and insignificant in their own home.

Screw that. Who cares if people are impressed with your house? It reminds me of the game we used to play when we were kids—King of the Mountain. You tussle and wrestle with the other kids to see who can stay at the top of the pile of dirt. Many of the goals people have in their adult lives amount to just about that.

Our challenge is to step out of this mindless conformity and away from the need to impress others and help save the planet from arrested development. We care too much about "arriving" at some predetermined place defined by someone other than ourselves. It's time for a rebellion, or better still, a self-directed creation.

The status quo had its purpose at one time. Mankind, at some lesser-evolved point in history, had this clan thing going, and if you were not one of the family, you were out in the cold with the saber-toothed tigers. We don't have that problem anymore. We don't need our neighbors' approval to survive. Although we're not meant to be alone, developing our individuality no longer carries such dire consequences.

What makes us individual and real beyond a few simple likes and dislikes? One of my favorite books, *The Urantia Book*, has a good explanation. It talks about the spirit within us, suggesting we each have a fragment of God that dwells in our minds with a perfect plan designed specifically for each person—depending on our genetic background, our culture and time, our mental composition, and all of the other things that make up an individual life. That plan is communicated, in large or small measure, through the creative insights that are gently presented to our minds as we go through life, trying to figure out the best way to approach any situation according to our highest ideals. Of course, just about everyone on this planet is so far away from being able to follow the "still, small voice" within us that we're pretty much guaranteed not to follow that perfect plan. So we have to improvise a little.

Discovering the real purpose for our lives can be illuminated by asking ourselves a few questions. One of the most basic questions we should be able to answer is: What kind of life goals should we be pursuing? Another is: When we take a look at the way things are done in our society, which parts of the status quo should we reject, and which parts should we follow? And last but not least for any SheBiker is: How do we create an outrageously genuine life while still living among the sheep?

What is the goal of your life here? The question is a lot easier to answer if you don't define your lifetime in terms of a scant 100 or so years. That's not your entire life, that's the first baby step in a long journey. "Life" goes on for millions of years—even eternity. During this journey, the physical is subordinate to the mind, which continues to evolve and refine until it achieves the ultimate goal of becoming spiritual. When the self is fully spiritualized, it becomes eternal, stepping outside of time to exist in eternity. Then the real adventure begins.

Life here on this planet is the first step in a relationship with a fragment of God that even now lives within us. Each of us is a unique variation in an infinite number of variations within a Divine Pattern.

That pattern is composed of all the values that humanity has responded to throughout the centuries, no matter what part of the planet they lived on. Those values are love, goodness, beauty, patience, courage, loyalty and other characteristics that are based in love and not in fear. The more we internalize those values and express them to the universe, the more real we become, because those values are the ultimate reality.

Some of those values are prevalent in society, and some of them are hardly considered by the general public at all. Which leads us to the second question, about deciding which parts of the status quo we should keep. Not everything about the status quo is wrong. There are plenty of "socially accepted" values in society that also reflect ultimate reality, because they matter to people everywhere, all the time.

But you knew that. You can't discard kindness toward your fellow folk. It will always be in the mix. Most of the rest of the status quo is optional at best. Sure, you can decide to make lots of money—as long as you don't toss out your integrity in the process. It's pretty simple to figure out. And the more you begin feeling and filling your life with the substantial worthiness of divine values, the less important the optional goals will become.

As you move forward in embracing more of the things that really matter, and become clearer regarding the goals of true substance that you want to achieve for your life, you may find you're moving somewhat against the flow of the general populace.

You may notice that you feel yourself rebelling against always being treated as if you belong to that ugly bulge in the middle of the bell curve. You may realize that many of the people around you seem to be incapable of responding to situations spontaneously, and they do everything based on what everyone else does.

When you start to wake up and everyone else around you still appears to be sleeping, it can require some patience and courage to continue developing a unique life, one that doesn't follow the path of the public at large.

Even though we may feel at odds with people around us, we have to keep developing our own paths. If we continue to contort our lives to fit things that don't really fit us, we lose out on the ability to be true to ourselves, and that means that one more incredibly awesome person will never actualize. It's enough to break your heart. A whole world of zombies, when we have so much to do and so many resources to do it with.

It is essential that we exercise the courage and maintain the proper perspective from which to feel our worth outside of how we "fit in." Instead of relying on the status quo, we can seek the spirit within us to give us our sense of value. We have to take that terrifying leap of faith and act on our belief in the things that we know, deep down in our gut, are true and good and beautiful. Truth, beauty and goodness, when integrated into our lives in substantial quantities, raise levels of self-respect far higher than any conformity to dead levels of standardization.

We don't have to rebel with anger. Rather, we can create with originality and disregard how it looks to anyone else. The people around us who may be unhappy we've decided to change the rules may be reacting unconsciously out of their own fear that their lives are based on shaky principles. We can take moments of conflict and use them as opportunities to demonstrate how the joy of being real can spill over into love for others. That's the way it's supposed to work. But relationships can present a challenge in how someone else thinks we should be and how we know we're going to be.

GEARING UP FOR THE RIDE

I GROW UP IN KANSAS, WHICH WAS NEVER THE EPITOME OF progressive culture. I think I had it a little better than most people, because I grew up in a household where both parents considered themselves equal partners. They had well defined roles that were very traditional in nature, but my mother was never subordinate to my father. By the way, my mom rode a motorcycle. It may have only been a Honda 50, but she rode it.

My father worked in advertising, and one of his accounts was a health club, a small Midwestern chain that had recently been purchased by a larger chain under the name of one of the founders of the fitness movement, Jack La Lanne. Every red-blooded American knew who Jack La Lanne was because of his TV fitness show, and I was even more aware of him because my father and mother were early fitness enthusiasts. They can still run circles around my lazy tush.

Jack himself came to town to promote the grand opening of the newly converted chain, and I rode in the car with my father to pick him up at the hotel. At the impressionable age of seventeen, I was excited to be in the presence of this paternal paragon of the exercise world. I sat next to him in the car on the way to the opening.

I don't remember what prompted his comment, but I distinctly remember when he announced that he believed women should be barefoot, pregnant and in the kitchen. I was a compliant little thing in a gentle society, so I was surprised by the ferocity of my reaction to his statement. Although I kept silent, I felt the heat rise in my face, and suddenly, Jack didn't appear to be such a great guy anymore. It was a defining moment.

My dad didn't agree with him either, but being the business host, said nothing. Besides, had it come to an argument, Jack would most likely have talked us to death, because that man had some stamina, let me tell you.

I can thank Jack La Lanne for changing my life, but in a way he would never have imagined. I still don't do my jumping jacks, but I can spot a sexist fitness guru a mile away.

Mr. La Lanne's comments really peg the issue surrounding a woman's desire to love and serve the people around her. I have a very mothering side to me, and it's taken me a long time to figure out how to serve others in loving-kindness without being taken for granted. If I show up in the kitchen, I want it to be a choice I make, not a duty I'm required to complete.

At one time, that might have been my chosen role. But women and men are both putting in 40- to 50-hour workweeks these days before they ever get to the housework, and statistics indicate working women are still doing the majority of domestic duties. A good place to start in our efforts to change that problem is to discover why we allow ourselves to be in that situation in the first place.

I can only make the decision to cook or not to cook if I believe I have that right. That's where a lot of us fall short. We may object to doing certain domestic duties, but we feel bound by some invisible rule that says we have to. We all know, in theory, that we have the choice, but in practice, we're still not consciously choosing. Sometimes we don't realize that the biggest barriers we have in being treated fairly are the ones we have constructed ourselves. Habits are hard to break, especially when they are passed from generation to generation.

It's often women's own perceptions that stop them from escaping limiting, traditional roles. I would not be so naïve as to say it ends there, but it always humbles me when I see the results of my intentions becoming manifest. Intention and belief are incredibly powerful. If we don't want to be treated as domestic servants, we must be very clear about the messages we're communicating to others.

But once we're certain that those messages are exactly in line with the way we wish to be treated by others, we sometimes have to work against the momentum of other people's ideas on the subject. That's where you really have to put your faith into what is true and real about the issue, and then speak up. Depending on where you live in the world, that could be all it takes, or that could be the beginning of a very long battle.

In the arena of intimate relationships, truth is where it all comes together. There is always a certain amount of give and take between two people, but truth has to be the standard to which we turn. If you're still out there in the never-never land of arbitrary manipulation through the use of sexual favors, or the use of the silent treatment for days, or whatever you may use as a means of getting your own way, seeking the truth of an issue may seem to be the long way around. Especially since truth is kind of subjective. But there are ways to get to something that reflects your understanding of the truth, which I define as being your best understanding of your highest ideals in any situation.

To start with, you need facts that are verifiable. Continuing with the kitchen analogy, it might go something like this: "We both agreed that we'd share the kitchen duties. We agreed to alternate cooking dinner every other week for the whole week. I didn't want to be fuzzy about this, so I kept track of how many times you actually cooked on the two weeks you were in charge of the kitchen. Both weeks, you only prepared dinner three times. Here, I wrote it down on the calendar."

You're stating facts. Unless you're using those facts as missiles, you'll be doing both of you a favor by being accurate about what happened. Depending on how long the issue has been going on or how many times you've had to bring it up, you may be able to move on to a resolution, or you may need to stop here and share something about how this makes you feel. When you share your feelings, you need to own them. You need to separate your feelings from his intentions.

Are you feeling angry? Then say so. Anger is a clean emotion. If you say you're feeling used, then you're implying he's using you. That may not be accurate from his side of the situation. If you say you feel he's acting as if his time is more important than your time, then begin with the words, "In my judgment." By owning your feelings without assigning their cause to him, you give him the respect and the space to respond.

Ideally, you're telling him how you feel to give him insight into your personality, not to assign blame. If his behavior makes you feel a certain way, regardless of whether or not it's his intent, then telling him will make him aware of how his behavior might trigger that feeling in you the next time he does something similar. It's just one of those little things that helps people who love each other get along better. If he still can't understand your reaction, then you might want to talk to a professional therapist who helps couples navigate these kinds of situations.

Once you've cleared your feelings, you can move on to resolve the situation. Tell him what you want. "I want to get back to the shared schedule we agreed upon. Would you be willing to do that?" Here, you're presenting what you believe to be the highest ideal in the situation. You're asking for how you think equality and respect should be present in the situation. Your significant other may have something to add that will modify this ideal—facts and wants of his own that will change what needs to happen.

When both parties start with facts rather than accusations and work respectfully toward the ideal, the whole relationship takes on a different dynamic. It's called sanity. It engenders passion, joy and peace.

If you can't get your significant other to accompany you into those effortful discussions about what is true, I don't know what to tell you. Good luck, that's what I can tell you. Been there, done that, divorced him.

People really don't talk much about truth as being a standard for relationships. That's probably because not many of us know what *is* true. Truth is what is real in the most ideal sense. When the truth of an issue is discussed with love and respect, it's actually possible to find a reasonable amount of agreement.

When you have to negotiate your rights in your personal relationships, it helps to have a standard on which both parties agree. The more you seek truth, the more often you see it, and the easier it is to use it as a guidepost for your life. You can't help but improve your relationship when you're both seeking the same thing, which also happens to be the high ground.

And it's the truth that we should engage in loving service, not as a way to get others to love us, and not as a way to build up our account so we can request favors in return, but because it's the right thing to do.

Truth and relationships are symbiotic. Relationships are not only a context for loving and receiving love; they are an excellent place for exploring and coming to terms with truth.

A relationship is an experience we can have that has no ceiling on it for excellence. A relationship can act as a testing ground for what is true and as a perfect arena for personal growth. The experience we have with another person attests to the validity of values we want to see actualized in the world at large. Relationships, of course, offer a host of other wonderful things that you can't experience any other way except with another loving person.

If a relationship is that important, that complete, then loving service for others takes on a certain dignity that should never be tainted with the feeling you've been imposed upon. Menial tasks can take on the level of art if the intention is noble. We must refuse to degrade our efforts by making certain that others do not take those efforts for granted. In addition, we have a duty to ourselves to wipe out any vestiges of victimhood we may be indulging.

Victimhood isn't always something we're indulging—there is no such thing as fairness yet on this planet, and in that sense, there are billions of victims. In the arena of social fairness, truth is only one of the agents needed to evoke change. But in our personal relationships, we have much more leverage: we can expect to create results, or we can end the relationship.

In the dynamic of personal relationships, identifying ourselves as victims can be a crutch—an excuse for not taking risks, for not putting much effort into hopes and ambitions, or for keeping commitment at arm's length, just in case we're "being duped"— which keeps us from taking responsibility for our own happiness. As long as we attribute our lack of actualization to the other person without really trying to live the life we desire, we're only cheating ourselves.

I've come a long way from being the Midwestern girl in that car with Jack La Lanne so many years ago. I've tried the kitchen as a way into men's hearts, and it works, but there can be complications. I like the fact that my new husband never expects me to take kitchen duty, and that he appreciates my efforts just as I appreciate his.

I didn't speak out against the domestic ball and chain in my past marriage and silently resented the hell out of the situation. I thought I was doing everyone a favor by not starting a fight, especially because I knew there was always one waiting for me. Instead, I kept my mouth shut and my love died. It wasn't a good trade.

Defending what we know to be true is an arena in which we have to exercise faith. We don't have to push our will on someone when we believe in what we stand for; truth has a power that stands on its own. Speak up with the grace engendered by honoring what's real. Even if things don't work out the way you want them to, you're still on the right path.

Truth is a powerful ally. By aligning ourselves with the truth day after day, we receive the validation of what's right. This helps us avoid the urge to take petty actions that often accompanies problems we have in relationships. It helps to keep us on the right path when things get really crazy, such as when one of those relationships goes south.

Many of us will experience divorce in our lifetime—if not

directly, then we'll be affected by at least one divorce through someone close to us. What's the current statistic, 50 percent? And those are just the *legal* unions.

Ending a serious relationship can be so traumatic that it almost feels like too much effort to respond consciously to what's happening at the time. Divorce is one of the most intense episodes of life on this planet. It can really screw us up, or we can learn from it. The choice is ours. If we are going to develop into SheBikers, then this particular "birth by fire" is a perfect opportunity to see if the values we are relying on are worth their salt.

If you don't have children, divorce is awful. If you do have children, divorce is worse. When there are kids involved, you are seldom as removed from your ex as you'd like to be, and Lord knows the kids will never let you forget the fact that their lives have been changed forever. Just when you're feeling like a real loser for putting them through this mess, you walk up to the checkout counter at the supermarket and read a magazine's headline that says something encouraging like "Divorced Children: New Studies Show—It's Worse Than We Thought."

But it happened, you're divorced, and you're trying to raise kids in a way that isn't natural. Well, such is life. This is where we find ourselves.

Whether we can admit it or not, being in a divorce presents us with the opportunity to evolve our soulfulness. It challenges us to rise above our base emotional reactions and to handle the situation as the strong SheBikers we are becoming. I can't think of a more difficult episode where we have the opportunity to put our values to the test. Because let's face it—what good are all these beautiful qualities if we can't rely on them in the moments when we're emotionally exhausted, depressed, angry, sad and afraid? If things like courage, loyalty, honesty, compassion and patience don't work in this situation, then they never will.

One of the biggest challenges we face in a divorce is letting go of the act of revenge. Revenge has no place in your life. It's a disgusting, base reaction to injustice. You're better than that, even when you're angry. You're human, and the fantasies will appear in your mind, but your will is master over your mind, and you can repeatedly replace those thoughts with something more constructive. Just don't go there.

It helps if you can step back and view this nasty episode from a more extended perspective. When you look back at even the last ten years of your existence, and you think of all the things you've done, the people you've known, everything you've accumulated in memories, material possessions and wrinkles ... what do you have to show for it?

All you have to show for it is You. And whether you became more gracious and powerful, or more petty and bitter through it all primarily depends upon the way you perceived things. People go through similar experiences, but those experiences end up affecting them differently. That's largely due to the differences in personal perspective.

What's the secret to a good perspective? In a word, expansion. You're going to be alive in the universe for millions of years. When you really own that concept, you'll discover that even something as traumatic as a divorce takes on less frightening implications. It becomes different through your perspective. How important will all this seem in a hundred, a thousand, a million years?

No one should blow off her responsibilities. But all the petty nonsense that goes with the drama of a divorce isn't important. How you conduct yourself *is*, because that's what you are left with at the end of it. Sometimes that's *all* you're left with!

I heard something from a sister once that was very instructive to me. She said when she got to the other side of the really ugly divorce moments, she was grateful that she had decided to retain her dignity, because then she could look back at a very painful episode and know she had succeeded in walking her talk for love. She conducted herself in a way she could be proud of, even when the anger rose in her or her significant other was behaving in a less-than-dignified manner. Adhering to your values through adversity also helps to infuse some sanity into an episode that feels like you've gone to the other side of the moon and you're never coming back.

Your level of self-worth and your sense of safety make a difference in the amount of dignity you can muster when you're being treated unfairly, which is usually how we perceive we are being treated in a divorce. Get your strength from whatever source you call Divine. Because unfortunately, you can't always count on your friends or society to supply you with support when you're in the throes of a divorce.

I used to belong to the Wives of Bad Marriages Club. We didn't really call it that; it was just understood. We had various levels of denial; some of us just weren't in enough pain yet to start waving red flags. Some of us had crossed over the line into that twilight zone of dysfunction where we became cynical and started inflicting various and subversive power trips on our spouses in an effort to "make them pay." Some of us, myself included, became really good at living in a parallel universe where everything was fine. But since that wasn't a real solution, my mental health started to break down, which gave me another set of problems. I finally had to admit that I was allowing myself to go crazy because I wasn't willing to deal with the painful truth.

When I declared my intention not to live like that anymore, things got a little crazy. Some of the women in this group were very upset by what my declaration of honesty implied for their own situations. Some of them just stopped calling, others launched aggressive campaigns to prove me wrong.

You would never do those kinds of things, I know, but I guarantee you there have been times when all of us have been insensitive to the plight of our friends. It's important to realize that some of your friends will be insensitive, too.

At the very least, you'll separate the friends from the chaff. That can be a blessing in disguise. And you'll get to practice forgiveness. Like you need more chances to do that.

And by the way, do me a favor: If you ever find yourself at the beginning of a divorce, don't hire some lawyer with a reputation that guarantees he or she will viciously destroy your ex while you stand by innocently posing as someone who can't possibly understand the process of how this should all come down. That's just a subterfuge for revenge. There are some amazingly wonderful lawyers in the world, and then there are the other ones. You don't want anything to do with that karma.

Life is an adventure. Divorce proves how ill-equipped we are to live it. We make mistakes right and left. The bottom line is that when we get to the end of our lives, and we do some accounting of the successes and the disasters, we can be thankful there's a Divine Being who loves us even more than we love our own children. We may screw this life up royally, but we have millions of years for improvement. Seriously. You don't think God will make you justify your existence for eternity based on the merits of what you did in the past fifty years, do you? How unreasonable do you think God is? Would you do that to your children? Of course not! So relax. There's plenty of time to get it right.

But while we're on the subject of life's unpleasantries, our discussion would be incomplete without addressing that wonder of wonders: PMS, premenstrual syndrome.

My husband engages in conversations online with people around the world, exchanging ideas and expanding concepts in a fascinating global community of truth seekers. He tells me about the smart and interesting people with whom he dialogues, and often as not, the best discussions are with women.

I enjoy hearing how brilliant my sisters are, so he frequently shares their online posts with me. There have been a couple of incidents, however, in which the typical online etiquette of women writers has fluctuated drastically from their normal demeanor. Although cyberspace may be a fairly new forum for this phenomenon, it is a familiar issue.

Here's what happens: An online discussion becomes rather heated between a woman and another list member. These two individuals go back and forth over a period of days, politely arguing over a particular issue. Then one day, out of the blue, one of the woman's posts will be uncharacteristically venomous, lashing out at the person on the other side of the debate in a manner she hasn't displayed before. A day or two later, she'll apologize for the post, citing PMS as the reason for her nasty tone.

PMS is a difficult antagonizer to control. It is scientific fact that a woman's mental and emotional states can be altered during certain times of her menstrual cycle. I've experienced it, as most women have. PMS and other hormonal fluctuations create behavioral effects that women would rather avoid.

However, although my reactions may be over-the-top, the issues that come up when I am under the influence of fluctuating hormones are usually telling in another way, and far from being something I can only attribute to PMS. Sometimes the hormonal imbalance has just enough intensity to push me over the edge so I react to something that's been bothering me, something I should have brought up sooner.

I have to wonder if the women on the email lists haven't fallen victim to the same pattern, where they refrain from really speaking their minds, until one day they "lose it" and the resulting communiqué is much stronger than what they would have written if they had been more candid earlier on.

No, we wouldn't have said it that way in a normal state of mind. But when *is* it okay for a woman to stand up and say what's on her mind? When we do, it's often called whining, or bitching, or nagging, three terms people rarely use when describing the way men talk. Is that because men never speak their minds? I don't think so. I think it's because society in general still doesn't want to give women the right to react to or voice opinions about the issues that affect our lives.

Things have got to change. It is imperative that women own the reality that they have as much right to being taken seriously, to being happy, to having their needs met, as men do. Then our behavior during PMS will not be nearly as volatile. I believe that wholeheartedly. Women hold back their true feelings so much that when they experience the added stress of a hormonal imbalance, it often uncaps a torrent of pent-up emotion. Rarely does anyone in the medical profession even address this issue. PMS involves a lot more than just hormonal imbalance.

God intended men and women to be equally respected and regarded. The fact that women often blow up if we're hormonally stressed is proof that, for the most part, women are still not getting the respect and regard they deserve. But *we* have to make the change, Sisters. Now is the time to emerge as the awesome SheBikers we truly are.

A SheBiker is a strong, confident woman. But that confidence, that assuredness, isn't built on defiance. It comes from the calm dignity of a person who understands her worth. How do you become that woman? Don't look for support from society, because if you insist on getting your needs met, you're going to be branded as a troublemaker, not a heroine. Get your support from the Source, from God. If your concept of God is not developed enough to be a source of strength for you, I suggest you spend some time getting up to speed with that. Many of us rejected the idea of God that we grew up with, but we've been pretty sloppy about replacing it with anything else.

There are plenty of worldviews and religious belief systems that can be explored to assist you in catching up to a more adult understanding of who and what God is. I found an elegant and consistent portrayal of God in *The Urantia Book*. Not only did it give me a replete description of a Deity that made sense and didn't insult my integrity, but it also dramatically lifted up my regard for the entire human race. If everyone on this planet could get a sense of the value of a human being as described in this book, not only would we never question our own self-worth, but we would all treat each other with a startling affection and respect.

I know a lot of people feel uncomfortable when someone shares this kind of information and automatically label it "proselytizing," but truth never suffers from honest examination, so read it and decide for yourself if the book offers something worthwhile. You are important to me, so on the outside chance that you need help in recreating an adult version of the Deity we're dealing with here, I recommend you read *The Urantia Book*.

Many of us have found that meditation is an excellent way to bring us to the source of the conviction that we deserve to be heard. When you reach that place in meditation where there is no one but you and a loving Deity, you begin to realize there are no deals to be made, no roles to be played. The person you are, just as you are, is enough to justify the full inheritance of a child of God. Only when we experience the sense of worth that belongs to every person on this planet can we fulfill our destiny—to take our amazing SheBiker light into a world of darkness.

You have to believe, in your heart of hearts, that you deserve the rights of a whole human being. Because if you don't believe it, neither will anyone else. You may not be "liked" as much when you calmly tell someone no, you won't be quiet, you *will* be heard. We're in a tough time here, Sisters. Society doesn't reward women who insist on being treated well. Society rewards the martyrs. I don't know about you, but I think martyrdom is too high a price to pay for being liked.

Being a SheBiker may not be easy, and it's often not popular, but it's an excellent way to join the women who have come before us to blaze a path to justice, compassion and a better world. It's also a way we can decrease the inappropriate combustion of PMS and help the world understand that, when we are given our due each and every day of the month, there will be a lot fewer of "those days."

There will always be challenges in developing ourselves as strong, exceptionally independent, gracious women. As we successfully emerge as genuine SheBikers on the Biker Planet, we will also have to come to terms with the fact that we no longer fit in with "the crowd." That feeling can happen in many different situations.

I often feel like an outsider when I show up at my kids' school. Even though there are wonderful teachers and counselors who are dedicated to my children, I'm finding that I am increasingly at odds with the overall educational program.

Recently, I attended a meeting regarding one of my kids who doesn't fit into the mainstream mindset that's served by the public school system. At this meeting, the school staff suggested my child drop an entire subject to take another class—a nonacademic one—to help him better conform.

As I looked around the room at the meeting where this was being discussed, I noticed that no one seemed to be concerned that my son would receive no instruction on the academic subject being dropped for an entire year. "Wait a minute," I said. "How is he going to pick up next year with this subject if he completely misses out on the curriculum this year?"

"That shouldn't be a problem," came the answer. "Everything they are taught in the class this year will be taught again next year."

I felt my stomach tighten. Once again, I was confronted with the image that looms in my mind of the whole school system as a giant ruse—something we have put together so we can send our kids off with some vague sense of purpose, but with little of value actually being learned. And if you don't fit into this narrow system, what you learn the most is: You don't fit in.

I could be vocal about this, and I am—with sympathetic teachers and administrators, and with parents whose kids also struggle with the system. But we can't object too loudly. We'd be considered antagonistic and unsupportive, and the system is so huge and bureaucratic that change is next to impossible. Reforming the educational system is not my chosen passion, so I do what I can to make it work for my kids. But I can never feel at home there.

There are other places where I feel like an outsider, such as the conservative Christian church my parents attend, or a Halloween party at a neighbor's where the children's costumes have been handmade by enthusiastic suburban mothers.

But in those cases, I'm just misplaced. There are different social trends developing that really make me feel like I'm on the wrong planet. These trends are not the kinds of things you see on the evening news reports of the really horrible injustices that happen around the world. These are the things that happen in my hometown that just plain weird me out. Such as the way people are working harder than ever so they can go out and buy a bunch of stuff they really do not need. Or how so many people talk with really loud voices on their cell phones in restaurants or movie theaters as if that's okay. Or how they are so engrossed on the same phones while they're driving their cars that they pose a threat to me when I'm riding my motorcycle. Or how we're all gaining so much extra weight that we don't fit three across in an airplane anymore. Am I crazy? Are we not distracted beyond our ability to cope? I think something needs to turn around.

As awakened individuals, no matter how unappetizing the rest of the world is beginning to look, we have a certain duty to perform. We cannot be in this world without trying to bring it closer to what we know it needs to be. To that end, we need to dedicate ourselves to changing the world, even in small ways, to take society a little closer to the ideal we see in contrast to the way things are now.

We can't change the whole world overnight. But we have to start somewhere. We can develop a certain fragrance about us that can influence the attitudes of the people with whom we come into contact. I use the word *fragrance* because there has to be something attractive about change in order for it to be effective.

If we are to help move the planet's consciousness forward, we have to completely embody a new paradigm of thinking. We have to become walking billboards for evolution. There may be other personality types who are better leaders than we are, but we can all be leaders if we become vivid examples of what we know the world can become.

As we begin to project something that is often at odds with the rest of society, we will become outsiders. Being an outsider can wear on a person after a while. It helps to develop a group of friends who support your outsider ways. That means you have to stop relying on being acceptable to the status quo for your sense of worth. Develop friends who may not agree with your every opinion, but who aren't frightened by the fact that you don't "fit in." Find them on the Internet if you can't find them in your hometown. Look for other venues for validation. Subscribe to magazines that explore thoughtfulness. *Utne Reader* is a good one, *The Sun* is another (*www.thesunmagazine.org*). And of course, *Ms.* Magazine is better than ever.

Join discussion groups. Put some effort into building a world around you that gives you comfort in knowing you're not the only one who thinks differently. You're going to need this support because, as an outsider, you've awakened to the fact that things need changing. You can't turn back.

Being an outsider gives life a certain edge that doesn't allow us the comfort of settling into a space where we feel accepted by those around us. So what. Our stay on this planet is so brief. If we can create tension between what is and what should be, we can be instrumental in pulling our world's culture forward. There will be time to rest later. Being a SheBiker is not about being a bad-ass. But it is about living life in a way that's closely akin to riding a motorcycle: moving through space in a way that commits you to the experience in spite of the risk, and the feeling of power that comes from that. There is a thrill to having the decision in the palm of your hand to pull back on the throttle and cut through the air, being deliciously aware of reality as you speed through it.

Just like the Biker, we have the power to initiate momentum in our lives. Creating momentum with social and spiritual change can feel just as good as a motorcycle ride on a perfect afternoon. If you pull ahead of the pack for a while and feel like an outsider, well, so be it. You've given the others something to focus on.

And now, let me end the chapter with a little story. Because there will always be one essential component in this topic of change that must be present, or nothing we discuss will ever make one bit of difference.

One day, the Princess of Persuasion was walking through her beautiful garden. It was a lovely day, full of sunlight and warm breezes. The birds were singing and, well, you get the gist of it. Presently, the Princess came across a young woman who was sitting on a garden bench looking rather glum. It was one of the Ladies Who Are Always Waiting. There are a few of those in every kingdom.

"Why so sad?" the Princess asked of the Lady.

"I'm bored," said the Lady Who Is Always Waiting. "Every day I do the same thing. Nothing exciting has happened to me in so long, I'm beginning to believe this is the way it will always be. When I was young, I thought I would grow up to have adventures! To fall in love! But all I got was this lousy Waiting job and Friday nights with some guy who's nice enough but nothing to really write home about." She sighed deeply. Then she remembered that she was on the kingdom payroll and blushed for dissing her job. She smiled weakly at the Princess.

The Princess ignored that last comment and looked at the Lady for a long time. "What exactly did you have in mind for your life?" she asked.

"Oh, I wanted to be a singer," said the Lady. "But that was a ridiculous dream. There are so many people who sing much better than I do. I ended up getting a job at the village music store instead, and then the Royal Pain met me there and offered me this professional Waiting job. I knew the benefits would be better than what they had at the store, so here I am." She sighed deeply again.

"Why not take up your singing career again?" asked the Princess.

"Oh, no! I could never do that!" exclaimed the Lady. "It's too late. No one's ever heard of someone starting a singing career so late in life. I'm in my mid-thirties now, and it's pretty much just Waiting it out from here." The Lady Who Is Always Waiting looked at her watch. "Oh, my. It's time to Wait again. I must go." And with that, she got up, bowed to the Princess, and walked away.

As she walked to her Waiting job, she thought about her conversation with the Princess. "If I had been a Princess, I might have been able to be a singer instead of Waiting," thought the Lady. "She can do anything she wants." That made her even more depressed.

That night, the Lady had a dream. She dreamed she was on a stage in a spectacular amphitheater made of solid crystals, and an orchestra was playing beautiful music behind her. The audience seemed enthralled by her very presence, and when she began singing, to her surprise, she had an incredible singing voice. The moment was so exquisite that it transcended anything she had ever imagined in her waking thoughts.

The dream was a very vivid dream and was so startling that it woke the Lady up. She sat up in bed and decided she had to have the opportunity to really experience what she had dreamed of. She quickly got up, put on her Waiting clothes, and hurried out the door of her cottage and down the path, deep into the woods. Presently, she came upon the old cottage of the Witch of Wishful Thinking. Of course, being a witch, she was awake even though it was the middle of the night.

The Lady knocked gingerly at the door. The Witch was used to middle-of-the-night visitors, because that's when people get desperate and go out looking for magical answers.

As the Witch ushered her inside, the Lady put her case before the Witch. "I always wanted to have an exciting life, but it was not to be," said the Lady. "My fate led me to a pretty good Waiting job, but I'm thirty-five years old now and I feel trapped. I need a magic spell to free me from this life and into something better and more rewarding."

The Witch of Wishful Thinking rolled her eyes. She wondered

how so many generations of mortals could live their lives and still not figure it out. But what the heck, she made a good living off of their dilemmas.

"Come to the fire, Dearie," she said. The Witch never called any of her friends by that name, but it seemed to fit the role of her job, so that's what she called her clients.

The Witch sighed a dramatic sigh. "I would change your life into what you want, but I'm afraid you can't afford it," said the Witch. "An exciting, rewarding life is very expensive these days." She looked at the Lady out of the corner of her beady eye.

"Oh, I'm willing to do whatever it takes!" exclaimed the Lady, who was getting very excited just thinking it might be possible.

"Well, perhaps we can work out a payment plan. My heart has been touched by your plight. I'm willing to let you pay this off over the next five years," said the Witch, as she rubbed her long chin. "But! I will not allow the spell to begin in earnest until the payments are almost finished. So don't expect any changes until I have received the majority of the payments. And over the next five years, you must follow my instructions to the letter, or the whole agreement will be null and void, no matter how much money you're sending me. I'll know, of course. I have my ways." The Lady nodded solemnly. This was the part the Witch loved the most. She would have made a good used-carriage salesperson.

Into the wee hours of the morning, the Witch and the Lady worked out a payment plan that stretched out over the next five years. Next, the Witch lit some incense and pretended to go into a deep trance. When she opened her eyes, she wrote down a few things on a piece of yellow parchment she had imported from the next kingdom for this very purpose.

The Witch then held the parchment in her hands and, in her best mystical voice, slowly read the "sacred mandates" that the Lady would have to follow in addition to making the payments over the next five years.

The mandates included taking singing lessons at the Royal Music Academy, practicing an hour a day, going to Talent Night at the local pub every weekend, and dropping the deadbeat boyfriend.

As the dawn began to awaken the sleeping forest animals, the door to the Witch's cottage opened and the two women stood in the doorway, bidding each other farewell. As the Lady turned to leave, she looked at the Witch with glistening eyes.

"I can't thank you enough for helping me," she said quietly, almost reverently. "If something changes and I come into some money, I'll try to pay you off more quickly."

The Witch just smiled and nodded. Let's hope *that* doesn't happen, she thought to herself as she watched the Lady walk away down the forest path.

4

GOING YOUR OWN WAY

SEVERAL YEARS AGO, MY MOTHER HAD OPEN-HEART SURGERY. She had never had anything seriously wrong with her before, so it was a tremendous shock to our family. I got a phone call from my father and immediately flew home to be with them.

At the time, I was living a life that was less than perfect, and less than happy. But I was complacent about how bad things really were, and I had tricked myself into a pattern of hopeful living, as strange as that sounds. I was letting life go along its mediocre way without summoning up the courage to change anything, and I was placating myself by hoping it would get better. However, I had no idea how that was supposed to happen.

When my mother was wheeled back to her hospital room after her surgery, my father and I stood there and gazed anxiously at her small, pale figure, which suddenly looked so fragile. We were afraid—afraid for my mother, afraid of the unknown, afraid that she'd never be the same.

As I looked down at my mother in her hospital bed, a strange feeling crept up on me, like a wave of reality that was washing over my body. I was suddenly struck with the realization that I could be in the same place in a matter of years. My life could end while I was patiently waiting for something outside of myself to make my life different than it was.

It was a vision of my own mortality, and I was shocked to realize that I was wasting a perfectly good life that also happened to be a little shorter than it was the day before. I was dutifully standing outside of my own life, being someone I wasn't, waiting for permission from some outside authority to allow me to change into the Real Me.

I went home and made some hard decisions. At the hospital, I had confronted the fact that no one and no thing was going to improve my life for me. I could no longer go back into denial. You know the pop definition of insanity—doing things the same way but expecting different results? For the first time, that wasn't so funny. I was living an insane existence, and I wanted to change it.

Turmoil permeated my life as I declared my intention to stop trying to please everyone and, instead, live according to my own truth. It was an interesting period. I had no idea it was going to be so hard to be the same person on the outside that I was on the inside. A friend told me that the reason it was so difficult to turn my life around was that I had gone so far down the wrong road. It's true. Anything you do for a long time that isn't in your best interests or puts your personal rights at an extreme disadvantage can take a lot of energy to reverse. Just a few months before this all came down, I was given a surprise party for my fortieth birthday, and the cake had a caricature of me dressed up like Mother Teresa, with the words "A Saint at 40!"

Well, this saint lost her divine status in the community shortly after that. I turned my world upside down. Not that I really wanted to, but that's how far I was from being myself. Everyone around me had to adjust, and they complained loudly.

The most dramatic change was that I left a bad marriage, which I was just as responsible for ruining as my partner was. But I soon learned that apparently, leaving a marriage is something that's allowed only when it's decided by committee. Everyone I knew wanted to have some input on that decision, and they voiced their opinions without reserve.

There were other things that were irritating my friends. I was preoccupied and not available for them the way I had always been. I was no longer a convenient package in our social circle, but a loose cannon, a rogue. People had to expend effort to try to figure out who I was now, and whether it fit their own comfort level of someone they could relate to.

There aren't that many people who are willing to stop on a dime in the middle of a relationship and let you do that. But to be honest, when you start behaving differently, a few things are bound to alter. Sometimes old friends don't fit into your world anymore.

People who are accustomed to using you as a dumping site for their negativity will find you're not so indulgent as you once were. The little digs they normally make about the ways you behave that make them uncomfortable because you're not enough like them will begin to feel unreasonable and insulting to you. Hence you'll find other things to do with your time. All the signals they give you that say they don't quite accept you for who you are will turn into such big red flags, you'll wonder what you once found so fabulous about them that made you contort yourself to be acceptable to them. At the same time, you need to check that you're not involved in the same attitudes toward them.

When we go through major changes in our lives, we tend to be in some sort of altered state for a while. Some people call it a "mountaintop experience" or "battlefield euphoria." Just for the sake of keeping the peace in your sphere of family and friends, you may want to hold off on delivering those brilliant insights that have suddenly become so obvious to you, as you may be closer to indulging in self-righteous condescension than providing helpful advice. But that's only a suggestion. It could also be that you've finally found the courage to tell someone the truth. Your call.

I thought a lot about certain long-term friendships I was discarding, and I came to the conclusion there is nothing inherently virtuous about keeping friends for a long time if they don't feed your soul. When two people have a deep, abiding respect for one another that allows each to accept the other regardless of how differently they grow, now that's a friendship worth keeping. But when someone gets ticked off at you because you're changing right before their eyes and it's not happening in an orderly manner—well, how much value does that relationship really have in your life?

But there are other relationships you don't want to discard. It's important to let loved ones know you hear their fears about the changes taking place, even if they can't define what's happening. Change can create some strange power struggles for a while. But even though you may hear some objections, this change is not up for vote. Possibly for the first time, you are asking for what you need, you are saying what you feel, and you are making choices based on what you believe to be important, not necessarily what earns you the most brownie points from those around you. You haven't abandoned your relationships, but now, you've put yourself into the equation.

If you've always been out front about your needs, then you may not understand what I'm talking about. But if you're like the vast majority of women, you haven't been up front about your needs. You've created a life where you take care of everyone else, and if there's anything left over, you'll allow yourself a few crumbs from the table. When you finally realize that such a habit is a big contributor to your level of unhappiness, you can't go back. Once the veil is lifted and you realize you have to get what you need to be a sane person, you have to commit to going all the way with it. Respect, consideration and sensitivity to the fear of the people around you help earn their trust that you'll still love them after the dust settles. But you can't back off.

And as you slowly morph into the Real You, your goals will change. Your idea of what is important will start to focus more on what you stand for, and less on getting the approval of others. This authenticity is where your power comes from, my dear Sister. God has created you to ultimately evolve into an incredible spiritual child with the nobility and birthright of a full-fledged citizen of the universe. We have a teeny, tiny spiritual embryo growing inside of us. As we mature, and as we go beyond this mortal life, that embryo will eventually become the spiritual center of our identity, and that's a beautiful, beautiful thing. But for now, all we can do is try our hardest to pay attention, from time to time, to that gut feeling that helps us evolve.

Becoming more aware of that authentic seed of identity deep inside of us is the way to our greatest happiness and our greatest effectiveness in doing something meaningful for the planet before we take off for parts unknown.

We can become better and better at identifying with our real selves, and to some extent that's what the rest of this book is about. I've outlined a process and a mindset that focuses more directly on your ideal identity. Yours can be a gradual, exciting awakening, but you may have some birthing pains like I did, depending on just how much you aren't being honest with yourself. If any part of you is experiencing the discomfort of not being who you are, you've got to move off dead center. Our world is in so much chaos that we have no right *not* to get in touch with that authentic power and do what we can to leave this a better place than we found it.

You may be living the same hopeful, unhappy existence I was living. Or you may have come a very long way only to realize you're still as far away from your dreams as you ever were. It doesn't matter what financial or social class you're in; we can all relate to these problems. Most of us believe our lives develop the way they do and there's not much we can do to change them once significant decisions have been made, such as getting married, having children or spending years following a particular pattern. We believe that others who have had happier, more rewarding lives were simply lucky enough to be in the right place at the right time to take advantage of what the circumstances had to offer.

That's simply not true. The reality is, arbitrary circumstances rarely line up enough times to make anything significant happen. If we want to achieve specific results over a lifetime, we have to continually make decisions and take actions that take us where we want to go—we can't rely on fate. I wish the Queen SheBiker really did exist, but, unfortunately, life changes are made on the inside, not on the outside. Get rid of the idea that if only you're good enough—good student, good daughter, good wife, good mother—life will just make those tough decisions for you, remove all the risks and hand over your ideal life on a silver platter. This isn't grade school anymore! Real life doesn't give out rewards for obeying the rules. The big rub about all the contortions you put yourself through when you conform and obey is that, overall, you don't get much for it but a bad back. Sure, you might have a better chance at staying warm and dry, but *so what*? You're still living someone else's version of your life!

Create your own direction, your own vision of what life could be, and you'll have the chance to be truly alive. Living a life that is mainly in response to others puts you at a great disadvantage— your happiness is dependent on the circumstances and people around you. That type of life doesn't take you in any particular direction, and you have no control over the results. When you live in a reactive mode, life goes along its way without anything necessarily occurring that gets you closer to your interests, passions or dreams. In terms of expanding and developing your own inner brilliance and inherent God-given gifts, it's possible that nothing of significance will ever happen that way.

In the business world, the reactive mode is embodied in a job called "administrative assistant." This is a position where you are paid to support the decision-makers around you, and to do the grunt work that frees them to be creative and direct the goals and activities of the company. You do not initiate your own work except in being skillful at helping someone else succeed.

That's not a bad thing—there are many talented, creative people who are administrative assistants. But to them it's a job. This is your life! If we look at the analogy again, and see the company as your life, you should be occupying the position of CEO of SheBiker, Inc.

Somehow, we got the twisted idea that following our own call to greatness means we aren't taking care of the needs of others. We are often so identified by our roles as respondents to others— mother, wife, daughter, friend—that we are practically allergic to having an identity of our own. But, we may say to ourselves, isn't service to others what life is all about? Yes, of course. The dedication of the servant is a noble attitude that would aptly describe the lives of many of the world's greatest people. Dedicating ourselves to something greater than who we are is not only what needs to happen right now, it is the real secret behind a satisfying life.

However, there's a distinction about great people and people who are just responding to the needs of people around them. The difference is that most great individuals augment an attitude of serving others with a personal vision, something they have created and directed, which allows them to give the world their talents and brilliance. They commit themselves to a vision that reflects the fundamental essence of who they are, and they shape it into a picture of what they want life to be for everyone, including themselves. As they become walking personifications of their vision, they inspire and invite others to see themselves in the vision.

Being passionate about a compelling picture of a life that reflects who you really are doesn't mean you have to be a great leader. What makes a person truly great is a vision so transforming that she becomes something more than who she was. We are all capable of those types of visions—the difference is that some people actually live them.

My first husband came from a family of very strong women. His cousin, we'll call her Susan, was a powerhouse of a woman, who made an incredible contribution to her city because of a vision that made her more than she was. Her daughter was born with severe disabilities, and Susan spent the first few years trying to find services in the large city in which they lived that matched the vision she had for her daughter's life. Susan wanted her daughter to have ample opportunity to develop as an individual of meaning, to be able to build self-respect and a sense of value in her place in the community.

There were no such services in their town, so Susan made the decision to dedicate her life to implementing her own vision, not only for her own daughter, but for other children who needed the same services. She had to learn new skills, put herself out in the community in new ways, and discipline herself to make time in an already busy life to undertake an enormous project.

She founded an outstanding preschool for disabled children. It became a model for other schools around the country and was awarded many times for its excellence in reflecting exactly the vision Susan had set out to achieve. Susan slowly and painstakingly extended the preschool into an elementary school, and then into middle school and high school. She worked her tail off to fund it and hire teachers who were not only capable but compassionate.

When her daughter became a young adult, Susan realized that something needed to be done to assure her daughter would be in good hands after Susan died. Again, nothing in the area came close to the vision of what she had in mind. So Susan began designing a self-sustaining community for the disabled, a place where a cottage business could support those who lived in its community as they grew older. If those services had already been available, I have no doubt that many other ideas would have come to that brilliant woman's mind on how to make a difference in the world.

An essential vision of how we're going to kick some butt on this planet has to come from deep within our genuine selves. Whether or not it's the kind of thing that moves people to join you is not important. What is important is finding that passion within you and committing to it in such a way that it takes hold of *you*. It has to transform the life you are living now in such a way that you make a difference in the world. Creating your vision and living it will give your life more meaning, more satisfaction and more self-respect.

If you don't take the time to figure out what you stand for and exercise the courage to put it out there in the world, you may never feel you've arrived in your own life. May I repeat myself? You may never feel you've arrived in your own life unless you stop being what you think you're supposed to be and start living an authentic vision of who you really are.

Women are taught not to rock the boat. It would be very easy to spend the rest of your days doing what you need to do to "keep things running smoothly." You may wonder if change is even possible.

Change is very possible. Susan had a commitment to her vision to change the community for disabled children. I can't even imagine how much effort something like that would take to build from the ground up, but she had a clear, compelling vision and she wanted it so badly that she stopped at nothing to achieve it.

I would guess that you've instigated change before. Just think back to something you were so determined about that you were successful in creating a difference. It doesn't have to be a grand-scale event. The point is to remember a time in your life when you had the zeal of a fanatic, and you made your vision a reality despite the odds. Perhaps what is missing now is a clear, compelling vision that would make you want it so badly you'd stop at nothing to achieve it.

Living from a vision is a big transformation to consider. What we're talking about here is permission to pursue your dreams. Let's pretend you've just let a genie out of a bottle, and you know, without a shadow of a doubt, that anything you wish for can come true. What will you wish for?

Of course, you can't defy the laws of the physical universe, but the power behind the commitment of a clear vision is a force to be reckoned with. If you wait until the time is "just right" or until someone gives you "permission" to become the awesome SheBiker who is languishing inside you, you'll never achieve it. There are women who cannot imagine that their dreams are important enough to upset the balance of all the things already going on in their lives. They think they'll wait—until their current crisis at work is over, or until their children reach some magical age, or until (you fill in the blank).

The SheBiker inside you needs to get out into the world. She has dreams and passions that can make a difference on this planet.

It's time those dreams and passions saw the light of day. If you commit to an inner vision that represents your own passions and goals, your life will change dramatically and you will be able to give something real to those around you, something much better than what you are giving them now. You will live a genuine life that is a true reflection of the brilliance inside you. What's stopping you now is little more than a lack of commitment to an inner vision.

You may be rolling your eyes and thinking I must be daffy. How could I possibly say there's nothing stopping you from living the life you desire? I could sit and listen to you talk for hours before you would run out of reasons why you can't live a life different from the life you're currently living.

I am not implying that if you really committed to it, you could instantly do anything you wanted to. Dreams can take time. My dreams certainly have, and there have been times when I have become discouraged, or apathetic, or angry that things have taken so long. But I know that when we commit to a vision, nothing can stop us.

Why now? Because life never presents us with the perfect time. Because every day the world is without the True You is another day the world is missing out on your contribution to make a difference in life.

Besides, living a life in response to the direction of someone else, or setting your life's agenda by the circumstances around you, has many drawbacks. A reactive existence loses out on a lot of the things a woman experiences when she is living her passion. When you're not following your own dreams, life can be incredibly boring. You may feel tired and lethargic all the time. You've probably developed a certain cynicism over the years. And you believe that regardless of your efforts, nothing you do makes a difference anyway.

If you've been living according to someone else's plan, chances are you'll have a hard time letting go of wondering who will take care of these things and these people if not you. When you embrace and commit to becoming more of who you are, a vision of what you need to do with your life begins to form, something that is bigger and better than simply responding to the needs of those around you—needs that may or may not need to be handled by you. Once you find your own passion and begin to live the life you desire, that amazing mind of yours will automatically begin to exercise one of the true mysteries of the human being: It can actually sort through the things you need to take care of, and discard the things you don't need to do anymore. And another amazing mystery? Somehow, the other things you always thought you needed to do will get done anyway by someone else, or they'll fall by the wayside as the unimportant pieces of fluff they really are. Isn't life wonderful.

Perhaps you're beginning to imagine the possibilities of living a life full of passion and substance. But you still may be uncertain as to how you actually accomplish such a transformation. It's much easier than you think. There is an interesting dynamic that takes place when you get clear about your dreams. When you commit to accomplishing the goals required to realize those dreams, the difference between where you are and where you want to be develops tension, like a rubber band that's being pulled in two different directions. Once you embody the vision of what you want in your life and *you commit to it*, your life will start being pulled in the direction of the vision. You will find that some duties and responsibilities are no longer as compelling as they once were, and that there is indeed time in your day to pursue other decisions and activities.

A new priority will rise to the top, and that priority is your vision of what you want your life to be. You will live your commitment to that vision in such a way that the people around you will have no doubts that you mean business. They may test you once or twice, but your commitment is much bigger than anything they've seen before. Surprisingly, everyone else around you will find another way to get what they really need.

Becoming a strong, powerful, authentic woman is the right thing to do because it's who you are, so it will somehow find its way into the scheme of things around you. You don't have to have it all figured out before you decide that these changes can happen. First, commit to your vision. Then, have the faith that the game plan will follow.

Committing to the emergence of the SheBiker inside you is something you have to own, it's not something you can "do." When I first went through the process of identifying what was of the utmost value to me and what I wanted to manifest in my life, the first thing I did was start "doing." I outlined projects and plans and to-do lists to make it happen. That's not the answer. First, I had to become very clear about what was important to me, and then I had to own it 100 percent. It is who you are being, not what you are doing.

You must *be* the walking embodiment of the things you value and the vision you hold. Then you "do." Anything you do before you own that vision wholeheartedly is just another worthwhile project. You need to change your entire perspective, not just take on another project.

Until you are committed to and personifying the worthwhile values in your life, your life will not change. This isn't about creating projects or even goals. This is about getting clear on what matters to you, creating a vision of what your life would be like if those values were completely present in your life, and then understanding how that vision needs to be expanded to include the whole world.

ON THE ROAD TO CHANGE

ALL THROUGH MY CHILDHOOD, I STUDIED THE PIANO. BY THE time I was fourteen years old, I was memorizing lengthy concertos and executing difficult music with a fair amount of mastery. But at the beginning, when I sat down that first day with my neighborhood piano teacher, I only knew that I wanted to play the piano. How it would happen was still a mystery to me.

I dedicated my time to practicing and playing. It was slow going at first. But over time it became easier for me to sit down with a new piece of music, open it to the first page, and begin teaching my mind and my fingers the landscape of this new terrain. After practicing and practicing, my mind and my fingers would become so familiar with the piece that I no longer had to think about it. Notes just "flowed" out of my head, into my fingers, and onto the keyboard. I was never quite sure how the process worked. All I knew was that if I worked at it, I made progress.

The assimilation of a new concept, technique or idea involves certain processes. First, you conceptualize the idea. You think about what it would be like to change the way you interact with reality; you consider a different way of being.

Then you take a hard look at where you are right now. Where you are at this moment in time is important because it's the place from which you're starting. If you're like most of us, there's a good chance you spend most of your time reacting to other people and outside circumstances. That type of life never gives you the opportunity to achieve significant progress in actualizing your dreams, nor does it allow you to create a direction that uses your unique talents and skills to make a difference in the world.

The act of "doing" does not bring about fundamental change in life; we need to embody the essence of value contained in the things that matter to us, and only then can we really expect to lead a life that makes a difference.

Fortunately, God takes care of most of this process. No matter where you go in the universe, you'll find that reality has been set up to favor progress. Our little mud ball of a planet is in the same flow of reality as the rest of the cosmos, regardless of how much it appears to be going absolutely nowhere. If you are clear about what you want, and you've grounded that vision in reality—values—and you commit to making it happen, then your brilliant mind and the indwelling spirit that gives you creative insight are all you need to make it happen. Your commitment, in partnership with reality and divine grace, will get your creative juices flowing. If you take responsibility for doing your part, then just as it did for me as a piano student, the progress inherent in the way God set up the universe will do its part to move you forward.

There's a reason it's important to consider all this in such a deliberate way. A particular kind of energy is released when you're really clear about where you are and where you want to go, and it's the secret weapon for making things happen. It's a creator's type of focus, one that makes tools and open doors stand out from the rest of your environment. I first learned about this kind of creative energy from author Robert Fritz in his book *The Path of Least Resistance: Learning to Become the Creative Force in Your Own Life*. Fritz calls it creative tension, and he describes it as the force that comes into play when we are standing at point A, seeking to travel to point B. The tension is caused by the difference between the two points, in the same way that tension is created when you pull a rubber band in two directions. If the rubber band is attached to two different objects on a slippery surface, and one object is much larger than the other, that rubber band is going to resolve its tension by drawing the smaller object toward the larger object. If your vision is greater than your current reality, the tension will naturally pull you toward your vision. If we set up the situation correctly, our lives can't help but move forward in the direction of our dreams.

You may have had a different experience in the past. You may have tried to change things, only to find yourself right back in the arena of How Things Have Always Been. Most of us are familiar with this yo-yo dynamic. Something happens in the world and you feel that inner nudge to get involved to make things better. The Queen SheBiker is giving you a thump on the head, but you don't know where to begin. You make an enthusiastic and energetic start, but then you look around and realize you're drowning in a sea of have-to's, and you know you'll never get beyond your dutiful existence to create an outrageous life and participate in changing the world.

Not so fast, Sister—that change is possible, and you don't have to figure out how it's all going to happen before you start.

One of the reasons we feel so powerless to make sweeping changes in our lives is that we are "doing" instead of "being." The project mind-set is a crippling habit that keeps us from really making a difference in life. The female mind is a great organizer, and it can assist us in reaching goals, but it also plays to that good-girl dysfunction of spending our lives helping everyone who appears to be less organized than we are. We are the gardeners who water, weed and feed everyone's lives. Well, tell those folks they need to do a little weeding and feeding for themselves. Whatever it takes, look up from your garden and set your view on the horizon. This is a time in our planet's history where we can't stay in the comfort zone. SheBikers need to get very involved in what's happening around us. We do not have the luxury of watching the world go by.

Simply taking care of the things that present themselves to us will not create a large enough vision of what we know life can be. If that vision isn't substantial, it's difficult to maintain creative tension to keep moving forward. We must embody the values contained in the vision we seek in order to have a strong anchor into the future. Once we've created that stake in the future, and we've got a clear idea of where we are now, we've got the tension we need. Like you need more tension. But this kind is a little different.

The dynamic of creative tension begins by being crystal clear about where we are today. This involves an honest assessment of our lives. We have to look objectively at the protective strategies we've developed over the years that keep us operating in a limited arena of life. These strategies keep us in a comfort zone that prevents us from growing or becoming anything more than what we already are.

Think about those protective strategies as a ditch we dig for ourselves. This ditch represents the beliefs, habits, attitudes and reactions that we adopted somewhere back in our lives that probably worked well for a particular situation when we were younger, but don't adequately work when we unconsciously turn to them now in other circumstances. Instead of being out in the bright sunlight interacting with life on ground level, we spend a lot of time down in our ditches. It's familiar and comfortable there. Kind of like digging a foxhole in a battlefield. You know you're not going to get shot at if you just stay down in your comfort zone where you're safe.

Ladies, we must move beyond the comfort zone. But to assume we can do so through a sheer act of will is a recipe for disaster. The only way we can move beyond where we are is to get clear about what matters to us and to commit to embodying the values we are passionate about. That commitment, when we see it in contrast with the way things are in the world, can be compelling enough to make us move away from our safety zone and take some ground in our lives and in the world.

After we do climb out of our safety ditch and move toward our dreams, we will run into barriers—fear and vanity being two of the greatest. That's when you need to be really clear about what you stand for. It will help you keep from running back to the ditch, help you face barriers and move beyond them, especially as you begin to move away from acting in ways that give you approval from others. You can't rely on the world to encourage you here. What will happen instead is that society will pull you back into the comfort zone. Watch out for the Approval Whore. She's lurking deep in your psyche, and she'll combine forces with the status quo to hold you back, if you don't pay attention.

Your anchor in the future is made up of your authentic brilliance and the values you stand for. If you commit to becoming real and value-driven, God will give you that push you need to make it out of the ditch.

Creative tension is a dynamic you will use from this moment on to achieve results. It really is a gift from God. If you can learn how to set the scene needed to put this tension into play, it will unconsciously take you wherever you want to go. You can become an expert at developing creative tension so it becomes the automatic force you use to achieve all your dreams.

Inherent in the ability to access creative tension is an acknowledgment that there is something greater in life with which you interact. If you really think you're on your own, you're dreaming. SheBikers are powerful creatures because they make full use of their connection with a Higher Power. Don't ignore that connection just because you happened to be handed a load of hooey in your religious upbringing. Institutional religion can be a paltry shadow of the real thing, which you can access directly. Experiencing creative tension is a good exercise in getting familiar with the will of the Divine Creatress.

One of the most essential aspects of setting up creative tension is a realistic assessment of where you are today. It's very important to establish this sense of current reality. If you wanted to ride your motorcycle to New York City and you didn't know if you were in Cincinnati or Nashville, you'd have a hard time getting the right directions. Creative tension is your road map. You have to know where you are to get to where you're going. Where are you right now in your life?

Realistically assessing where we are is not something we all do very often, because we have to face our shortcomings. The truth is, we are all amazingly adept at overlooking glaring problems—not so much because we're good at forgiveness, but because we just don't want to deal with the negative aspects of our lives. Well, I'm not asking you to get real in one fell swoop, but I am asking you to at least exercise the courage to admit to where you are and what your current state of affairs might be. If you don't, you'll be like the woman who doesn't know if she's in Cincinnati or Nashville. Current reality isn't something we need to beat ourselves up about, but it's important to acknowledge where you are right now. Then you can focus on the horizon and get going.

This is so vital that I'm going to suggest you ask friends and family members who know you well to write down a description of the Current State of You and their observations of the way you react to life. This is a great exercise. People are always willing to help with this sort of thing, and your fear of hearing negative things will usually be overridden by your desire to hear cool things about yourself. Try it—rather than hearing something new, you'll most likely just get confirmation of what you already know. But it's an essential body of information for any serious SheBiker as she heads out to change the world. Know thyself, Babe.

Here are some good questions for you, and for your pollees:

What are my strengths and weaknesses?
How do you see me reacting to difficulties?
What methods do I use to solve difficulties?
What are some words or phrases you would use to
   describe me?
Do you consider me a big-picture person or a detail-
   oriented person?
What things appear to be most important to me?
Do these jeans make my butt look big? (Just joking,
   skip that one.)

If you have spent years carefully developing an external image of yourself that isn't really you, it may be difficult to find a handful of people who really do know you. The very thought that some-one might actually see through your smoke screen can be very discomfiting.

The effort to conceal who you really are may be the most lim-iting protective strategy you have. It's a common one, for both men and women, and it begins at an early age. It's certainly some-thing I fight against even now. People can spend so much time creating a persona they want people to believe that they never get around to developing who they really are.

There are many things about being a woman in this culture that can trip us up. If you were raised as I was, you may have been taught to be nice and likable when you were growing up. It's a common family curriculum in America. Consequently, many of us seek approval as our means for change. That's one of the biggest differences between the ability to be effective and the rut of wishful thinking. You must wean yourself from relying on approval, because being approved-of is not the same thing as being effective.

Getting approval from others has very little to do with realiz-ing your dreams. Instead of concentrating on being likable and pleasant to be around, and getting your way through methods of manipulation, develop the skills and values that put you in a position to be powerful. In other words, create value in what and who you are. That makes it inevitable that you can get what you want, because you can command it. Don't rely on others to give you what you want because you're just so darned cute.

Even though we think we're fooling the people around us, enough of our real self comes through in our behavior and atti-tudes that people probably know us better than we think. Don't be afraid to make the request that people assist you in this self-assessment. If they are friends at all, they will be eager to help you.

This also creates another dynamic that is important in the "real-izing" of your dreams. You can't commit to a vision of who you want to be and what you want to see made manifest in the world until you are willing to be vulnerable in that commitment. You don't have to announce your plans to everyone, but don't hide them. Acknowledging your commitment helps the endeavor become more real. Get it out of the safe and cozy arena and move it into reality. If you are keeping it under wraps, are you really committed to making it happen? You could be sabotaging yourself from the very beginning if you don't wholeheartedly engage in the effort to make this change. Vulnerability is also an inevitable result of being instead of doing—who you are needs to accompany what you do.

The assessment you and others are going to create is also very helpful in understanding what your protective strategies are. Once you become clear about what you do that keeps you from overcoming barriers in your life, you will be better able to identify situations that keep you from becoming the person you long to be. These need to be faced head-on.

For example, I really hate confrontation. I will give up practically anything to avoid it. If I have a goal and someone is standing in my way with awkward confrontation written all over them, I will simply decide, in a variety of sophisticated denial tactics, that my goal was wrong/not worth it/stupid anyway.

Admitting this to myself has helped me tremendously. Instead of turning tail and running pell-mell into my "ditch," I have had to hold my ground and create a strategy to navigate through this scary territory over and over, until I now own the technique that offers me a level of success. I still don't enjoy confrontation, but it doesn't hold nearly the power over me that it once did.

I also understand that I am a big-picture person. That's fine, but there are many instances when I am faced with all the details required to actualize my grand ideas, and I try to avoid them. Or I do a really sloppy job and then wonder why I'm not achieving my goals. Consequently, I need to balance that aspect of who I am so I have the skills I need to accomplish my goals.

More than fine-tuning our skills and overcoming particular faults, we need this picture of our current reality so we can set up the tension needed to actualize our dreams. It's not that examining and reexamining our faults makes us transcend them; it doesn't. Instead, it's like the maps they have in shopping malls on those big boards—we need that big X that says "You are here" before we can figure out how to get to our destination. Then, we embody the values that are inherent in the ideal vision we have of our world, and this embodiment will be the impetus that moves us forward in overcoming those faults and changing the world.

To continue this self-assessment, spend some time going through your memories of your achievements and failures. It's a very helpful exercise that may accomplish a self-assessment more quickly than any abstract gathering of characteristics. Events can contain snapshots of ourselves that reveal the most about who we are. Some people like to write in journals, and if you do, this would be an excellent exercise for your writing. Others don't like to write, and if you don't, then go for a ride on your motorcycle, or a walk, or find a comfortable place to let your mind wander. (You *are* going to get a motorcycle, aren't you?)

One interesting aspect of looking at achievements and failures is how they have colored the way we see things. Using the example again of my piano playing, I know that my achievements with music early in life gave me the perspective that, if I was persistent in any undertaking, I could be successful. That perspective has supported me in accomplishing my aspirations in life.

On the flip side, when I was a young adult and first moved out on my own, my big-picture thinking and lack of attention to detail caused me to repeatedly run out of money. Instead of seeing this for what it was, I developed the perspective that money was some mysterious thing I wasn't any good at understanding. This belief made me dependent on others for my money management, which resulted in all sorts of negative complications.

The power of perspective is a dynamic not unlike the one in which people simply respond to others without directing their own lives. If we are unthinking in our perceptions, if we simply allow thoughts to rise in our minds and act on them without challenging the truth of our own assumptions, we are again limiting ourselves. Just because we have a thought, attitude or emotion bubble up to the surface of our consciousness at a particular moment doesn't necessarily mean it's the most appropriate one. Consider instead that you might be better off choosing the thoughts, attitudes and emotions that move you forward toward accomplishing your vision for the world.

There are many examples of people who have transcended debilitating perspectives. Viktor Frankl is one of them. He is a very important character in the history of humankind. He said, "One of the last remaining freedoms is to choose one's attitude in any given set of circumstances." He demonstrated the power of perspective in a way I hope to God fewer and fewer people will ever experience on this planet. Viktor Frankl was a prisoner at the Auschwitz concentration camp during World War II. He survived, and he wrote the book *Man's Search for Meaning*. That he chose to love and forgive his captors and tormentors while enduring such horrors remains one of the most incredible examples of human spirit the world has ever known.

Frankl is a stunning symbol of the power of perspective. I tell you of him here to clear the air of any possible belief that we are victims of our circumstances.

The most debilitating perspective a person can adopt is seeing her life as being under the control of the things and people around her. Frankl witnessed hundreds of fellow prisoners who lost the will to live, because they saw themselves as victims of an evil regime. They crumbled under the cruelty of their treatment. But Frankl, who was as much under the control of his captors as the other were, refused to grant his captors entrance into the inner sanctum of his soul.

Day after day, Frankl continued to see his life in the concentration camp as a story he would recall in the days to come, when he was reunited with his wife, when he would teach again, when his circumstances would return to a sane and just existence.

If you believe that your life is filled with problems that need to be solved, that will be your experience. If you see yourself as a victim of circumstances, you will have great difficulty taking charge of your own destiny and creating a life that matters.

Back in the 1970s, I was a teenybopper in love with a ridiculous band called The Monkees. I can still imitate Davy Jones's little front man jiggle, although only when I'm really feeling silly. But the band did have at least one authentic musician, named Michael Nesmith.

Besides doing some amazing things in the music scene, Michael recorded a very interesting album called *The Prison*. It was written by a young, idealistic artist who wanted to communicate what he observed about human nature. The album is a story instead of a collection of songs. The story is about a community of people who live in a prison. The main character is a young man who has lived in the prison all his life and has known no other existence. But one day, he decides to attempt an escape, and through a terrifyingly dark night, he wanders about in pitch-black nothingness, unable to see where he is going. Determined to continue, he finally sees a dim light in the distance. He collapses, exhausted, and the next morning, awakens to find that others who have also escaped the prison have taken him in. But what they tell him is something he can't believe, and he returns to the location of the prison to find that their story is true: People are moving around in an open space in total freedom, acting as if they are locked behind prison walls. They are prisoners only of their own beliefs. So limited are they by their own thoughts that they actually see prison walls where there are none.

When we commit to a vision of what we want in our life, those limitations begin to fall away. The trio of mind, reality and divine grace is a great committee when it comes to finding creative ways of making something happen. Just like the prisoner who made the decision to escape before he really knew what was waiting for him outside the walls, we have to exercise the faith that there will eventually be a light in the darkness, and that a way will open up for us.

Faith actually has a lot to do with a healthy perspective. Faith is a belief that you hold to be true, so much so that you are willing to base your actions on it even when circumstances don't support that belief. When you are stuck in a prison of your own making, you have to take a leap of faith that your commitment to another way will yield results. Once you identify the values that define your vision, and you embody those values in a whole-hearted commitment, there are no circumstances strong enough to stop you from making yourself and everyone around you the recipients of your worthwhile dreams.

Believing we are somehow limited by our past is a debilitating perspective. We may wonder: If we haven't been able to achieve a goal before, why should we believe we could accomplish it now? But if that were true, no infant would ever walk, no athlete would ever break her own record, and no musician would ever become a virtuoso.

Perspective is not the same thing as an affirmation, nor is it a brainwashing activity to make you believe things are different from what they really are. You can't "wish" your way into change. The change that needs to take place in your life will require planning, detailed execution and tenacity. But it will never come to pass if you don't first allow yourself to create the vision and commit to living it. If your perspective is one of powerlessness, you'll already be convinced it can't happen.

Learning to create change can take time. You may find it hard at first to believe you have the power to make a difference in the world. But I promise you, as a person who has gone through this process of change, it's only a matter of time before you realize that your dreams can become reality.

NAVIGATING BY VALUES

MY FRIEND ANNA GREW UP WITH AN ALCOHOLIC FATHER AND a mother who did her best to hold things together. It was the 1950s, long before Twelve Step programs were popular, and long before people understood how alcoholism and codependency issues passed from parent to child. By the time she was sixteen, Anna was an alcoholic, too. As a teenager in the '60s, she left home and married another heavy drinker. She began her "adult" life repeating mistakes she had learned as a child, while she created a few new ones of her own.

There was plenty of substance abuse, and Anna's husband physically abused her. The marriage lasted long enough to produce two sons, and when Anna finally ended it, her ex-husband didn't seem to care much about what happened to her or the boys. Anna began the arduous process of overcoming her alcoholism, raising two young boys, and struggling with a life of unresolved psychological issues that are the result of the chemical imbalances that often plague physical bodies on this planet.

Anna always worried that she wasn't the best mother she could be. But she had worked through the twelve steps of becoming sober and rediscovered the things in life that were most important to her. She taught those values to her sons. She tried hard to model the things she stood for, always living as an example of what she believed in, even if those choices didn't create the easiest solutions. She only hoped that her faith in the ultimate power of goodness was a perspective her sons would carry with them into their own lives.

As the years passed, the two boys were growing into the kind of people she hoped they'd be, and her life began to reflect the hard-earned progress she was making, too. Her oldest son was grown and on his own, and the decisions she made now around her living situation were all about creating the best environment for the last few years that her younger son, Joey, would be at home. She tried very hard to make up for all the things she felt she had put him through.

One day, when Joey was about fifteen years old, he called Anna at work. In a shaky voice, Joey told her that his father, Anna's ex-husband, had just called on the phone. Joey's father was a distant figure in his life. He still drank heavily, and the few times Joey had been around him, his father had never exhibited interest in developing much of a relationship. But now Joey's father wanted him to come live with him and his wife 200 miles away, and he intended to fight Anna for custody.

Anna felt the familiar knot tighten in her stomach, as it did every time something more went wrong. It seemed that her life was a long list of things that went wrong. She didn't understand why Joey's father was suddenly insisting that Joey move to be with him. Whatever the reason, it was unexpected and unsettling.

Joey didn't want to go anywhere; he was happy where he was, perhaps for the first time in his life. After a rocky start, he was finally doing well in high school. He was on the football team. He had friends and decent grades, and his life was working. Anna heard the fear in his voice. They hired a lawyer, who assured them Anna's ex-husband didn't stand a chance of getting custody. They believed him.

Several weeks later, Anna found herself in a courtroom hearing the judge read a letter she had written to her ex-husband two years earlier, when Joey was struggling at school, asking her ex for help in dealing with their son during a time when Joey was frustrated and uncooperative. That time had passed, and things were going smoothly now. But her ex-husband's lawyer was using the letter as the centerpiece in a story that presented Anna as a woman who was incapable of raising a troubled son. The lawyer requested that custody be awarded to Joey's father, claiming he was more capable of handling Joey.

Anna's attorney hadn't expected the other side to take that angle, and he scrambled for a way to counter the strategy. But it was too late; the judge decided that Joey was too much for his mother to handle, and awarded custody to Anna's ex-husband.

"I just sat there. I didn't want to look at Joey," Anna told me. "When I did turn around and look at him in the row behind me, he was sitting there banging his fists into his head, and he began to cry so hard I thought he would lose his mind. He said, 'Dad, Dad, don't do this' over and over. My heart was breaking. I felt I had let him down, once again. He just kept saying, 'Why? Why?'

"I went over to him and put my arms around him. We both knew his father had lied. I had always told Joey to tell the truth, and now we were being manipulated by lies. It wasn't fair, but we had to respond in a way that reflected our values, not his father's. I said, 'Joey, we can do this. We can do this.'"

Joey's father sat across the room looking stunned at the judge's order; perhaps he had been trying to prove something and now he had inadvertently gotten what he'd asked for. For Joey, it was a sentence to spend years of his life with strangers in a strange place.

Anna watched through tears as Joey got behind the wheel of an old Chevy his grandmother had given him and dutifully followed his father on a four-hour drive down to Nebraska, where he would live for several years in the basement of his father's house, away from his friends, his dog, his football team, and the life he and his mother had worked so hard to create. For a fifteen-year-old who had already been through so much, it was a difficult thing to agree to do.

"Before Joey left," Anna said, "I hugged him and I said, 'You know how to do this, you've got to do it, Joey. I've taught you. We will always be connected.' An attorney told me, 'Anna, here's what you can do, you can go down to Nebraska, drive the boy to the state line, have him get out and walk across the state line, and that's all there is to it.' I told him, 'I brought this boy up to know there is a better path, and I will not undo that.'

"I was mad. I was terrified. It was two years of the most unbelievable pain. I'd drive down after work on Friday to be with Joey for the weekend. When I'd get there late at night, he'd already be at the motel waiting, and he'd stay there with me. I would have to leave on Sunday. We would just hold on to each other, and I would see that kid cry again. I would say, 'Always remember I love you and I'm with you.' He'd write me letters, saying things like, 'Mom, I saw a flicker today, that's your bird, so I knew you were with me.' I never prayed so much in my life, in hopes that my energy would go down that highway to that boy. I learned to pray at work and in the middle of the night; I learned that God is very real.

"After it happened, I felt like I was being punished, although I had tried so hard to do the right thing. I thought: What's this five years of sobriety about? What did I do wrong? I took it to the bare bones of my soul and found out it isn't about punishment. It was simply about not knowing. There was a lot of not knowing how to pick a healthy relationship, and taking my children through a lot because I didn't know I wasn't sober yet, that I hadn't worked through all my problems. It was about not knowing if I could trust that the values I was telling my children would give them the strength to handle whatever came their way would actually be enough [to do that]. What I know today is, it is exactly enough.

"I watched that young man get through those years just like a trooper. I hoped that someday Joey and his brother could forgive me for everything I had put them through because of the choices I had made in my life. I knew God was real when they said, 'Oh, Mom, we forgave you a long time ago. You need to forgive yourself.' I knew I couldn't deny the existence of a loving God any more."

Anna now has a career through which she offers her strength to other women who struggle as she did so many years ago. "When I'm talking with women about custody battles and they ask me what I think will happen, I tell them, 'I don't know, but I know that there's a God who listens, and who goes into the courtroom and will give you the strength.' And I tell them, 'First and foremost, you be there for that child.'"

Joey met his future wife at the high school he attended while living with his father. They moved back to the town where Anna lives, and Anna now has a beautiful granddaughter. Anna's older son lives in town now, too. She recently married a man who treats her with respect and shares her abiding love for her sons. "I've got it all," Anna now says. "The circle comes around. It's what I tell clients: It's a God thing—I have no doubt.

"We need to hang on to something here as things shift and change. Women are coming into a place of knowing that they have the strength it takes to make it through. We just need to stay true to what we believe is right."

Life presents us with opportunities to be very clear about what we stand for in our lives. Anna had to make a choice—she found herself in a situation where she needed to show her son that they could rely on the truths they valued to get them through. She knew what she believed, and she wasn't going to use a different set of values to find her way through the tough times, even though others might have used such heartbreak as an excuse to stop taking responsibility for their lives. Anna had already exercised tremendous courage facing the hard facts of what her life was missing. She was familiar with the place inside of her that could provide the sustenance to get her through another ordeal. She taught it to her son Joey and she modeled it, and today he reflects that same commitment to the values he holds as central to his life. Instead of passing on the disease of alcoholism, he will live as an example of this precious lesson for his daughter.

God doesn't sit up in the clouds somewhere concocting ways to make us miserable so we can learn hard lessons. God's design of reality is so exquisitely consistent that when we live life in denial of what we know is true, we can find those brick walls without any problem all by ourselves. For those of us born on the Biker

Planet, pain is often the defining experience we go through before we learn that lesson, whether we set it up for ourselves or not. Sometimes, like Joey, we're affected simply by being a part of the human race.

When we don't live according to our ideals, we do horrible damage to our personal integrity, because we force our minds to make up something to justify our inaction, and that takes us a little farther away from being real. And then, of course, we're also not standing up for what we believe in, so the world loses another chance at having the tide turn, one molecule at a time, toward a more sane existence.

One of the reasons we're so wishy-washy about our values is that very few of us ever really get to know the values we say we believe in. If you haven't thought through why loyalty, for example, is such an important value to you, you might not be moved to rely on it when the opportunity presents itself. Once we become well acquainted with the qualities of a particular value, they become much more attractive to us.

Sometimes life forces us to test out the things we say we stand for, the way Anna was forced to rely on the values she stood for. But if we're fortunate enough to avoid the heartache that often becomes our teacher, then to arrive at that clarification, we have to care enough to allocate the brain waves to do the work voluntarily. We are wasting a perfectly good life if we spend our days in a comfortable fog, never really being clear about what we believe in.

It's true, ignorance can be bliss. A person can live a relatively happy life without ever defining what it is she stands for. But why would you want to spend your life that way? You are an amazing SheBiker, and you know in your heart of hearts that your unique perspective, strength and wisdom could make a huge difference on this ball of mud. You deserve to design a life of compelling purpose which utilizes your unique talents and skills and feeds your soul. (Don't forget, you also need to save the world.)

You can begin designing a fabulous life for yourself by being clear about the things that matter to you. Why? Because inherent in the things that matter to you is your purpose in life—kind of like the fortune in the cookie. Figure out what lights your fire, and it will lead you to your destiny.

What matters to you? Most of us spend so much time on the surface of our lives that our answers would be pathetic in the larger picture. But that can be remedied. You just need to stop and think about it. The problem with that is, once you've stopped to think about it, you may feel the need to change things. It's easier to just keep distracting yourself with a bazillion and one things in life, the way most of us do by staying as busy as we are. Are we accomplishing much of lasting import? Probably not. But who has the time, right?

If you're going to continue with me in this book, you need to realize that I'm here to change your life. This isn't a feel-good book about personal and spiritual growth. This is a kick-butt book about bringing you back from the Land of the Consumer Zombies, or helping you fend them off, at any rate, so you can more effectively do what you need to do, which is awaken the SheBiker inside and love the world into a saving grace.

But here you are, staring down the road at another twenty, thirty, fifty years of the same thing you're doing now, and as much as you desperately want to have a purpose that makes a difference in the world, you've got no clue as to how to make that happen. The first step is to reacquaint yourself with the things that matter to you—not to your spouse or your family, not to your girlfriends or your community, but to you.

What matters to you? When people answer that question, they may say things such as financial security, good health, good relationships, or making a difference in the world. Qualities like the ability to make "courageous loyalty" or "patience and understanding" come up less often. Neither type of answer is wrong, but the differences are important. We tend to see things that matter in action, in doing, in tangible or at least measurable quantities. The *source* behind good health or the ability to make a difference in the world is the less-explored arena of values.

Values are not something we immediately think of when we consider what is important in our lives. If I asked you if honesty is important to you, of course you would say it is. But it's not necessarily something we consciously work on in our lives. When we're young, we're taught about values in a "Don't" way. Don't lie. Don't steal. Don't, don't, don't. What an attractive presentation of the things that matter. Just thinking about it makes you feel like you're back in grade school. I doubt seriously if any of us was ever introduced to the essence of honesty and how imbibing such a glorious quality would feed our souls. Instead, values were pounded into our heads as morals. Sometimes morals make sense, but more often, they are akin to behavior modification. And they are often slipped into a sacred rules-and-regulations category, where they don't belong.

Perhaps it's time to see values in a different way than how they were presented to us as kids. It may be the first time you've revisited the topic of values as an adult.

Why is it important to see values differently? Values are more than a "Do" proposition. We often think they are limited to considering how we manifest our behavior—because it's the "polite thing to do"—it's how "good people" treat each other. But they go much deeper. When you drill down through the things in life that offer meaning in a deep, heartfelt way, it all boils down to these realities.

Anna went through the Twelve Step program and honestly confronted the shaky premises that had been holding her life together. By following the steps she was able to work her way back to the things that really mattered. When you reconsider *your* life, the best place to start is at its essence, at the values that matter to you. Look through the following list and circle the words that represent values that really speak to your heart. If you don't find the words here that best describe the values in your life vision (and believe it or not, that happens rather frequently), bring in your own words. This is an important process, so I hope you'll stay with me here.

Abiding	Calm	Deliberate
Able	Capable	Delicate
Accepting	Caring	Dependable
Achieving	Centered	Deserving
Active	Certain	Determined
Actualized	Charismatic	Developing
Adaptable	Charitable	Devoted
Adept	Clear	Dignified
Admirable	Committed	Diligent
Adventuresome	Communicative	Direct
Affectionate	Compassionate	Discerning
Aggressive	Compatible	Disciplined
Agile	Compelling	Discriminating
Altruistic	Competent	Diverse
Ambitious	Confident	Divine
Amorous	Connected	Down-to-earth
Artistic	Conscientious	Dynamic
Aspiring	Conscious	Eager
Assured	Considerate	Earnest
Authentic	Consistent	Eclectic
Authoritative	Constructive	Ecstatic
Awake	Contemplative	Educated
Aware	Content	Effective
Balanced	Contributive	Efficient
Beautiful	Cool	Elegant
Believable	Cooperative	Emerging
Beneficent	Courageous	Empathetic
Benevolent	Creative	Encouraging
Blessed	Cultured	Enduring
Blissful	Daring	Energetic
Bold	Decisive	Enthusiastic
Brave	Dedicated	Ethical
Bright	Deep	Evolving
Brilliant	Definite	Excellent
Brotherly	Deft	Exciting

Expanding	Healthy	Learned
Expert	Hearty	Legitimate
Explorative	Helpful	Liberal
Extraordinary	High-minded	Light
Fair	Honest	Lively
Faithful	Honorable	Lofty
Family-oriented	Hopeful	Lovable
Fearless	Humble	Loving
Fine	Humorous	Loyal
Flexible	Idealistic	Luminous
Flowing	Illustrious	Lyrical
Forbearing	Imaginative	Magical
Forceful	Important	Magnetic
Forgiving	Improving	Magnificent
Forthright	Independent	Majestic
Forward	Individualistic	Masterful
Fragrant	Indomitable	Maternal
Fraternal	Influential	Maturing
Free	Ingenious	Meditative
Fulfilled	Inner-directed	Mellow
Generous	Innovative	Memorable
Gentle	Insightful	Merciful
Genuine	Inspiring	Mighty
Gifted	Integrated	Mindful
Godly	Intelligent	Moderate
Good	Interesting	Modest
Goodhearted	Intimate	Motivated
Graceful	Intrepid	Musical
Gracious	Intuitive	Natural
Great	Inventive	New
Grounded	Joyful	Noble
Growing	Just	Nonjudgmental
Guiding	Kind	Noteworthy
Harmonious	Knowledgeable	Nourishing
Healing	Laudable	Nurturing

Objective	Progressive	Righteous
Open	Prolific	Risk-taking
Open-minded	Prominent	Robust
Optimistic	Promising	Romantic
Organized	Prosperous	Rugged
Original	Pure	Safe
Outgoing	Purposeful	Sagacious
Outstanding	Qualified	Sane
Particular	Quick	Satisfied
Passionate	Quiet	Searching
Patient	Radiant	Seasoned
Peaceful	Ready	Secure
Perceptive	Realistic	Seeking
Perfect	Reasonable	Self-accepting
Persevering	Receptive	Selfless
Persistent	Refined	Self-respecting
Persuasive	Reflective	Self-sufficient
Pioneering	Refreshing	Sensible
Playful	Rejoicing	Sensitive
Pleasant	Rejuvenating	Serene
Poetic	Relaxed	Serious
Poised	Reliable	Service-minded
Polite	Religious	Sharing
Positive	Remarkable	Significant
Powerful	Renowned	Simple
Practical	Resilient	Sincere
Praiseworthy	Resolute	Sisterly
Prayerful	Resourceful	Skillful
Precious	Respectable	Smart
Precise	Responsible	Sober
Principled	Responsive	Sophisticated
Productive	Restful	Soulful
Proficient	Restorative	Sound
Profitable	Revered	Spirited
Profound	Right	Spiritual

Spontaneous	Tactful	Upstanding
Spunky	Talented	Valorous
Stable	Tame	Valuable
Steadfast	Tasteful	Venerable
Steady	Temperate	Versed
Stellar	Tenacious	Vibrant
Stimulating	Tender	Victorious
Stirring	Tenderhearted	Vigilant
Straightforward	Thankful	Vigorous
Striking	Thorough	Virtuous
Striving	Thoughtful	Vital
Strong	Thrilling	Vivacious
Studious	Thriving	Warm
Sublime	Tolerant	Warmhearted
Subtle	Touching	Watchful
Successful	Tough	Well
Succinct	Traditional	Whole
Suitable	Trailblazing	Wholehearted
Superb	Tranquil	Willful
Supportive	Triumphant	Willing
Sure	True	Wise
Surviving	Trusting	Witty
Sustaining	Trustworthy	Wonderful
Sweet	Understanding	Worshipful
Swift	Unique	Worthy
Sympathetic	Unstoppable	Zealous
Synergistic	Uplifting	

The next step is to reduce the list, thoughtfully, to half the words you originally chose, and then reduce it more. Get it down to three or four words that really capture the essence of what your heart tells you are the concepts or values that matter most to you. Write these words down and keep them handy because you'll need them in chapter 7 to help you create a statement that describes your overall vision of the world—a vision that is based on the commitment to something so basic, yet so inspirational and powerful, that your life can't help but be changed. If you base your life on anything less, you are cheating yourself out of the reality that contains a sense of fulfillment.

Values such as love, truth, courage, loyalty, honesty, beauty, and goodness are real. They are the essence of how we live and how we interact with those around us. Values are the same realities that have been at the center of human life since the first mortal walked this planet. Everything *of* value in our lives can be broken down to these realities.

And everything that is broken down can eventually be traced back to love. This is probably a good place to have this discussion, because love means so many different things to people. But it's the power you're going to use to change the world, so let's define just exactly what love is.

Let's start with what it *isn't*. Love is not doing whatever someone else wants just because they want it. It's not putting up with being treated like your feelings, needs and wants aren't as important as another person's. It's not excusing the same hurt time after time because the other person says he's sorry but obviously isn't. It's not indefinitely putting your life on hold while you do things for others that they could probably do for themselves, most especially if you're doing it because you think it's the only way they'll love you. It isn't racking up brownie points for some future withdrawal.

I don't know what you call all of that, but it's not love. Love has many facets, which, in their totality combine to create the brilliance of reality. Love is the most real of all things. It defines what our lives are and what the universe is made of.

Plenty of events prove love isn't always the prevalent power on the Biker Planet. We've got a disturbing history, and our world today is a reflection of that. But underneath the chaos is a current of something so profound that it touches every single life on the planet.

There has never been a race or civilization of people who didn't have love in their lives. Small children can love. Grouchy people can love. At least one man refused his country's crown for love. It is a powerful force in our lives that makes things change and happen. Even though love sometimes transcends the language required to communicate its effect on us, it is *real*. In fact, it may be the most real thing we experience.

To get a sense of just how real and powerful love is, I turn to *The Urantia Book*. There, I find many descriptions of love, starting with the fact that everything is connected. "Every impulse of every electron, thought, or spirit is an acting unit in the universe. The universe is a whole; no thing or being exists or lives in isolation." (UB 56:10)

It seems to me that if we're all connected at even an atomic level, socialization becomes the most powerful way to respond to reality. If we're all a part of the whole, then love, which *The Urantia Book* also describes as "the desire to do good to others," becomes the most powerful intention we can have or action we can ever take.

A perfect example of this intention can be seen in nature. If you look at nature in its purest state, you see a living community that depends on each member and its surrounding environment to survive. Each part of the system exists for its own purposes *and* for the purposes of parts around it. Like love, the symbiosis of nature takes the well-being of all the parts into consideration.

We may not know how to manifest love in human relationships with the elegant simplicity of nature, but just as all living things need sunlight, we need love, Sisters, we *all* need it. That need, in and of itself, should indicate that love is the greatest of all realities. It is the one ineffable substance that humankind must have to survive.

If you take away the craziness of the planet, you're left with people who want to care about each other. That desire is so strong that, despite all the madness, love slowly but surely develops in each generation and makes strides in the realization of human rights and dignity. If you think about all the leaders in the world who don't give a rip about anyone in their countries but themselves, the progress love has made in spite of them is astounding. If you think about how love personally shapes and molds each of our lives, it becomes even more so.

God loves us more than we could ever possibly love each other. One of the expressions of that love is the dignity She gives us as individuals. She holds our individual rights sovereign in our own lives. She works with us by giving us insight and offering her own opinion, but just like a loving parent who wants her children to grow, she also stands back and lets us get the learning the only way that it sticks, and that's through experience. She lets us make the decisions, although She knows what's going to happen anyway, and if I could explain that, I think I'd probably have a third hemisphere in my brain that operated outside of time and space. Since I don't, we'll just have to say "hmmmm." But the consequence of having free will is that we experience a lot of false starts and dead ends, and we are affected by a lot of people who, in the positions of power they hold, exploit *their* sovereign power over others. Does that mean God is not just or fair?

What that means is that we must consider life from an expanded perspective. Our lives will go on for millions of years. If we can only realize that we will eventually grow into incredible beings who will integrate our pain into a powerful compassion for others, we can stop expecting everything to have a just resolution here and now. We would realize that growth is sometimes painful, but never to the point at which the individual won't eventually recover. We have to trust that somewhere down the road, those painful experiences will be a jewel in the crown we wear as brilliant, wise, experiential beings.

Struggle is inherent no matter how materially smooth our existence. Anytime you're living in imperfection, there will be constant adjustments. The quality of love we bring to helping others is the ultimate beauty that will transform our planet. If we achieve perfection on this planet eventually and our struggles are over, well, I'm sure God has something more up Her divine sleeve.

So we commit ourselves to do what we can to bring justice and relief to the world, and we stand up for the rights of those who are weaker than we are. Like a person who grew up in the "school of hard knocks," we have a choice to make, and that is to grow wiser, kinder and more resolved through our experiences, or to join the herd and take what we can get. The truth is, what you can get by making the effort to turn a bad experience into a rich character is ultimately more valuable than what you can get by trading that character in for a few shiny baubles.

There are many ways to come to the realization of the power of love. When a person develops a life-threatening disease or has a close brush with death, she may well experience the unimportant things in life as starkly contrasted with the things that are important—and rededicate herself to the things that "matter" in life. At the top of that list is usually some form of love. But we all know love isn't only something you "do"—instead, it is an ineffable quality at the essence of our existence. It is easy to understand what it means to "be" more loving. That's characteristic of values and ideals—they can always be *personally embodied* as qualities of character.

There are many, many other values that also shape our lives. Although we rarely think about them, when we choose actions that contain value, those actions have the ability to give a transcendent quality to the way we experience life. They embody the essence of what makes life meaningful.

When you strip away the things about life that are variables in any society, such as possessions or lifestyles, what you are left with are values. Kindness and compassion matter to all people, everywhere, in every generation. Loyalty makes people grow personally and spiritually in China as well as Chile. Courage is revered in Alaska as much as it is in Alabama. We can say, then, that these values are what are truly "real" about life.

If you choose to base your life on values, you could say that you would become more real, because you would be concentrating on the pure essence of life. How it manifests can occur in a million ways—why limit yourself?

When an individual leads a value-driven existence, life is more real to her. She sees the possibility of achieving an experience of her goals every day. Her personality, attitudes and behavior are fluid but centered.

How does one become "value-driven?" We may agree that these qualities are important, but how do you interact with them in a way that changes your life? That's a difficult question for many of us, made worse by the fact that we are such "doers." Only in America could something as anal and ridiculous as the DayTimer calendar become so important to so many people. We are obsessed with cramming as much doing as we can into a day's time. Somehow we got the idea that doing creates meaning in our lives.

Doing is good—we need to actualize our potentials into the real world. But doing should be somewhere in the middle of a chain of events that creates satisfaction and meaning. Instead, we act as if doing, if done enough, can create the experience of being. Not true!

The development of an essential life plan begins with looking at what really matters to us. Once our values are understood and our purpose is committed to, then goals and results come into play. But before they do, values must be embodied. We must become a walking personification of the values we honor. Otherwise we are fooling ourselves into thinking that enough "doing" will change the way we are being.

If you have a goal of "doing," such as "spending more time with my family," that's worthy. But if you take that goal to its "being" state—which is "to be more loving and more aware of how I can connect with my family"—then you have expanded the goal to include the satisfaction you crave, which is to generate and feel more love in your family, not only to spend time with them. This new focus would create more opportunities to achieve that goal.

I have a beautiful SheBiker friend who announced one day that she was going back to college to get a second master's degree. She wanted to apply for another job higher up the corporate ladder, and she thought getting another degree was what she would have to "do" to get the job. Six months and several thousand dollars later, she quit her classes. She hated school. One professor even told her that because she was older, she wasn't as serious as his younger students and he resented the space she took up in his class. She didn't learn nearly as much as she had expected, and at the age of forty-five, she found the entire school experience much less impressive than it had seemed in her twenties. Gee, I wonder if that had anything to do with why the professor didn't like older students in his classes.

She had to rethink her plan. Backing into the "be" attitude, she realized that what she wanted was to "be" qualified to apply for the job she wanted. But since she was a good little doer, she had come up with the game plan before she really tried on the commitment of being qualified. Interestingly, what the university experience taught her was that she *was* qualified. She already knew half of what they were teaching, and she could easily gain the rest of the knowledge on her own. She put her resume in order, applied for the job she wanted, and got it.

For those of us who lack confidence, sometimes the experience of contrast—of experiencing what *doesn't* work for us—is the only way we can admit the truth to ourselves. Sometimes we honestly don't know any better; sometimes we aren't courageous or energetic enough to commit to being what we already know we can be.

Here's an example: I know what a healthy lifestyle is all about. I was a strict vegetarian in my twenties, and I learned a lot about nutrition. I live in Boulder, Colorado, where healthy living is the predominant lifestyle, as common as the bicyclists, runners, walkers, mountain climbers, kayakers—well, the list is as endless as the list of stores around here that sell expensive gear to active yuppies. There is no doubt in my mind as to how to be healthy. I can tell you all sorts of things about the benefits of soy, about how much a person should exercise, and how much more water you should be drinking than you are. Does that make me healthy? No.

Let's say I decide to "do" something about being healthy. I join a health club and show up Tuesday morning for an exercise class. I'm doing something about that healthy lifestyle. But after the class is over, I go out to my car and light up a cigarette (not really, I don't smoke) and pull a Snickers bar out of the glove box. Snickers satisfies. (Okay, sometimes I do have one of those.) Does that make me healthy?

I know about health issues. I can do things to be healthy. But am I there yet? It's not until I commit to a vision of *being* healthy that my life changes. Being healthy is so much more than a decision or two to "do" something. It's about realizing that, if good health is truly important to me, then I cannot be consistent with my values while not caring for myself in the many ways I decide every day to mess up my physical temple.

Even though I value being healthy, I have to *commit* to being healthy. I have to be willing to make myself vulnerable to criticism because I am going to be overt about my commitment. I'm not going to hide the fact that I'm committed to being healthy. You're probably familiar with how we hide things, just in case we fail? That way, we don't look like losers. As if no one else can relate. No, I'm going to put it out there and show the world I mean what I say.

As I become committed to being healthy, all sorts of things will change. Perhaps I'll decide to walk to work. When I shop for groceries, I'll replace my regular bag of Milano Double Chocolate cookies with a bag of those cute little carrots. And I may decide to go to decaf so I can sleep better, which is also something that will make me feel better. (Decaf! Did I say that?)

By "being" healthy, instead of just "doing" healthy things, I have expanded my ability to manifest the value of health into all sorts of places in my life. It began because I was clear about what mattered to me, and I committed myself to creating that in my life. How it turns out is never something I can completely anticipate.

Being dedicated to a value is one of the secrets to creating force behind vision. Vision is the creative outcome of a commitment to values.

My own personal vision is about engaging my true, authentic self in everything I do. I spent many years trying to conform to a model of a woman who wasn't me, trying to be interested in things I really didn't care about. Now I seek to be genuine and real, and to allow my own dreams and strengths to shine through in my life. In doing that, I become my vision. I am a SheBiker. I am committed to being authentic and therefore powerful. I am that right now—although I have many goals in that context that still need work. I have stripped away all of the intermediate goals and missions, all of the "doing," and I am down to the real issues of what it is I want to "be" in life. An important aspect of this vision is that it is based on fundamental values present in everyone's life. If the vision resonates within me as a worthy goal of what I want to be, then it follows that I see it as a worthy vision for every woman.

Consequently, I am dedicated to supporting other women in being true to themselves, believing in their own self-worth, and having the courage to do what moves them in life.

I don't do this because I think I "should." I do it because I'm committed to that vision so wholeheartedly that it's changed my life. As I experience the value of that vision, I become aware of the fact that this value is bigger than I am. Therefore I can't be dedicated to it only where it affects my life, but must become a walking personification of that ideal. That results in my encouraging others to find it in themselves. If this vision weren't something that had a universal value, then I would somehow be stopping short of the essence of what matters to me.

Values aren't just "do" propositions that further limit what you think you can do or be. They are the building blocks of reality that you can use to structure life to be a genuine reflection of who you are. They help you bring forth the best you can give to the world. Values are a creative force driving meaning and substance into your life in ways you can never anticipate. Only one thing is certain: You must commit yourself first to *being the embodiment* of things that matter. The rest will follow. The foundation of what you stand for must precede anything else if you hope to access a flow for your life. Jesus said, "Seek first the kingdom of heaven, and all things will be added unto you." That's really good advice.

CREATING A VISION THAT DRIVES YOU

YOU'VE PROBABLY HEARD THE STORY ABOUT THE WOMAN WHO hails a cab in New York City. She gets in, and the cab driver turns to her and says, "Where to?" And she replies, "Oh, I don't know. Just somewhere nice."

That's a good description of how focused most of us are about where we want to be going and what we want to be doing with our lives. Most of us find ourselves somewhere down the road in our lives at places we didn't consciously choose to go. The problem with relying on others to take us "somewhere nice" is that their description of nice may be different from ours. To the cab driver, somewhere nice could be the hot dog stand at 96th and 3rd, which probably isn't what the woman had in mind.

In addition to relying on others to choose our destination, we also do this thing where we think we have to fix everyone else's life so it's more pleasant for them, and if you've trained yourself to be that kind of person, considering what you want to do with your life as a self-directed decision is a very foreign consideration indeed. If you've been living an existence that mainly consists of supporting other people's lives, the thought of directing your own life is almost forbidden.

I remember times, growing up, when people would ask me what I wanted to do with my life. I was already so adept at being who I needed to be to get their approval that I really had no idea. My first husband described my dysfunction best. He said I was like a water skier being pulled behind a boat going wherever the boat would lead me. He didn't know how to get me up there in the driver's seat any better than I did. I ended up leaving him because I didn't like where he was driving the boat. It never occurred to me to that I could be the driver.

I spent the next thirty years getting really good at helping others. But I could have helped everyone a lot more if I had gotten really good at being myself. Why is it that we think our own agenda will be a selfish one, just because it may not directly address all the needs of those around us? Or perhaps the question is: Why are we so stinkin' addicted to the approval of those around us, to the point that we allow the needs of others to overshadow our own noble purposes in life? I mean, really, other than the very young or the incapacitated, who actually do need constant attention, the people we're "serving" could easily absorb half of what we do for them.

What would we discover if we took the liberty of developing ourselves instead of mindlessly serving the needs of others? Although the servant attitude is a noble goal, I don't think God ever intended us to throw away the gifts we have to give the world so we could sweep up after everyone else's party, unless we feel deep inside that our gift is to sweep. I've met a couple of women in my life who really felt that way, but overall, most women I know have other plans they'd like to pursue. Where those plans ultimately lead us, especially if we are value-driven, is to a more meaningful, more effective life in the service of humankind than picking up someone's socks every day because they know that if they don't, we will.

Most women are very process-oriented. We like process. It's creative, and it's a place where we can nurture others. The results don't matter as long as the love is there, we say. But if we're not clear about what we ourselves can create that will make a difference to others, then "knee-jerk nurturing" can take up all our time. I think it's like moving to a bigger apartment. Everyone knows that the stuff you own will expand to fill the space you've got. It's the same with responding to others' needs; if you're not focused about what you want to do with your life, then taking care of everyone else's details can easily become a full-time job.

That's okay if that's what you want, but is that what you want?

Women's styles of leadership and vision are badly needed in the world. Now is the time to be engaged in life at a level where we can feel the pleasure of getting really good at our own skills and talents, powerful tools that bring us satisfaction while we use them to change the world. We deserve the freedom to choose and the thrill of discovery. We really care about the world and the people who live here, just as our brothers do. We can benefit from taking the time to consider how we can best utilize our authentic selves in making things better instead of always putting ourselves in the supporting role of someone else's dreams.

So what do you want in your life? What do you want for the world? Every one of us has at least one inherent perspective or skill set that could change the world. If those talents are used in a way that acknowledges the urgency of making this wacky planet a saner place to live, they can change not only the world but our own lives as well. I'm not asking you to leap off into the unknown and deny your current existence. I'm asking you to think about the things that matter to you so you can start creating your stake in the future—in the world's future.

If you're waiting for God to tell you what She wants you to do, I wish you the best of luck. It's true, we have within us the perfect Guide, and every once in a while, you know there's something transcendent about the thoughts in your mind. But on a regular basis, most people would agree, the divine creative spirit that indwells each of our minds is hard to access. The term "still, small voice" is hardly accurate. How about "next to impossible to tell, maybe I thought that up myself"? Or "I really need an answer, God, why isn't one forthcoming?" If God spoke directly to me with an actual voice, then I would finally know the exact course I should take to have the most success in life, but I would probably be so dumbfounded that instead I would just spend the rest of my days in a stupor.

No, the chemical/electrical/biological systems in our bodies are so screwed up that we'll have to do it the Biker Planet way and wing it. Hell, my brain is so chaotic that I can't even finish a complete sentence half of the time. How do I think I'm going to be tuned in enough to hear God's voice? That's why it's important to think about the values that really move us. Values are time-space reflections of God that are the scaffolding of reality, and the truest, purest essence of guidance we can find short of stumbling upon a burning bush. So if truth is important to me, then I should exercise the mental stamina to figure out how I could manifest truth in my life. Or I could figure out what I would like to see happen in my life and in the world, and then distill the essential values from that vision. It works both ways, and it's something we should take the time to think about in our daily lives. When we get clear about what we stand for, we'll be in touch with the guidance we need.

Once you get focused on what you want to see happen in the world and you're clear on how you'd like to evolve as a person, use your values to guide you and creative tension to motivate you. You will then be ready to ascend to the Queendom of SheBikers.

You begin by getting clear about what you want. I've included some suggestions here to help you think along those lines. By the way, if you're one of those people who never actually follows this kind of stuff when you're reading a book, no sweat. The purpose of writing exercises is to make you think about these things. However you want to come to these answers will work just fine, as long as you spend the time to think it through somehow. Brain energy is something we need to expend more and more of, if we're weaning ourselves off of following the status quo.

1. First, write out a description of the life you would love to lead. Go ahead. It's not dangerous. But be serious about it. Include only the things you know you would do if you were given the chance.

   At the same time, let go of the limitations of what other people might think, or how you believe these desires would affect those around you. You can't anticipate the effect your dreams will have on others. You can certainly conjecture, but this is not the time or the place.

Think about it seriously. Make up a life you honestly would live if you had the opportunity and if circumstances allowed it. Create whatever "what ifs" you need to give your imagination permission to create the life you'd love without consideration of how you would get there.

Get as detailed as you possibly can. Include the place where you'd live, and describe it in great detail. Think about what you would be doing with your time, what goals you would be working on. Write a description of your relationships, and the group of people you would call your friends. Describe the larger setting of your community. Think about what you would be like personally and what you would be doing to interact with the world.

Create your life according to what you want, not what you think someone else would want for you, or what would impress your friends, or what you think is agreeable to your family. Just write down the life you would love to be living, being realistic about choosing a life you would actually live if you had the chance.

2. Write out a description of how the world would be different, but limit those differences to your top three priorities. Be as specific or as abstract as you wish. You might choose something as specific as the eradication of world hunger, or as abstract as everyone in the world really believing in themselves and understanding how valuable they are by just being a part of the human race.

3. Once you've done that, think over your life to date and list three things you've done in your life that you're really proud of.

4. Write about what you dreamed of doing when you were a child. Reflect on what it was about those adult roles or careers you found attractive then. Are those things still important to you now?

5. Imagine that you're a 100-year-old woman, writing a letter to an adult granddaughter. You know each other well, and there's nothing that you could reveal about yourself that would make her love you any less. Imagine that she has just asked you what you would have done if you had been able to live your life differently. Write down your answer as thoughtfully and completely as you can, projecting your life out as you can imagine it will follow from where you find yourself now. You are revealing yourself to yourself. You are coming clean for once, so honor the woman who needs to have these inner places acknowledged, and write it as you would write to a granddaughter you're proud of.

6. Write about what you would do right now if you found out you only had one more year to live.

7. Reread your answers and rework them if you want to. Forget what everyone else thinks and make it real for yourself. When you've finished, share it with at least two people. It doesn't matter who the two people are. It only matters that you get it out of your head and into the world, and you make yourself a little vulnerable by declaring what it is you've always wanted.

One of the twisted benefits we think we get from a life that doesn't engage our entire self is protection from failure and criticism. But loss of vitality is a horrible price to pay for such a questionable benefit. Your passion needs to get out into the light. People who always play it safe are boring and selfish. The world needs the Real You to participate in life and make a difference. Write out your answers without holding anything back.

=====

NOW THAT YOU'VE COMPLETED YOUR DESCRIPTION OF YOUR vision for the future, I'd like to stand here with you, step back from the picture, and take a good look at it.

How did it feel to write all this down on paper and then read it to someone? For many women, it's the first time they've ever shared those kinds of inner thoughts with anyone. For some, it's the first time they've ever allowed themselves to think these things all the way through. For a woman who has spent the last ten to fifty years of her life being in a supportive role in someone else's movie, the scenes you have just described can feel foreign—but, I hope, exciting and full of promise.

Unless you've written something that's never been actualized before on this planet, it's doubtful that anything in your description is undoable. Other people are engaged in lives that have events, places or people like those you desire to have in your life. You have the right to have those things in your life as much as anyone else.

You may never decide to go after everything you've written about, but I hope you will take some action on behalf of this exercise of creative imagination. It's important not to leave it in the realm of the imagination, because that can get a little creepy. We need to act on our ideas. Life is hard, I know, and we're all insanely busy, but taking tiny steps toward the things we desire and being persistent about achieving results can create important changes, if we will commit to making our vision real.

It can be an empowering vision, and it should be. There is nothing stopping you from achieving it. If you are clear about your vision, you'll understand the values and commit to embodying the values that support this future life. When that happens, creative tension will move you forward. Someday, you may look back at this book and remember when you read these words, and you'll realize how much life has changed because you knew what you wanted and you committed to making it real. Why not? And if not you, then who do you think has all the necessary easy, direct life circumstances to create these changes? You're it, Babe. You know it needs to be done. There will be time to rest in a few decades. Right now, you're the Woman of the Century.

Let's dig a little deeper into the description of what you want in your life. Reread your description and ask yourself why these particular things appealed to you. What underlies your desire to have this state of being, or these people, or this sense of justice? What are you looking for when you walk into that scene? Examine how the values you selected in chapter 6 come into play here. If you need to, refine your choices to better align with what you've written.

Practically everything you've written down can be distilled into a pure form of what you desire. By becoming clear about the essence of these desires, you can get to the heart of the values you're seeking, which helps fortify and anchor a vision. With this more complete description, you can set up the creative tension to pull you forward.

When you get clear about a vision, it sets up a baseline from which to explore other options. Other ideas and desires will occur to you that are refinements of what you have described. These, too, will help you discover the essence of what you are seeking. Nothing you have described in specific detail needs to be changed, but this exercise of getting to the heart of what matters will help you clarify even more of what it is you're after.

There are specific techniques that can assist you in staying on target with this transformation in your life. But embodying a vision is essential before you begin looking at the tools. Finalize another look at your three or four essential values that fit best from the exercise in chapter 6. You are now going to use them to create a three- or four-sentence statement that expresses your overall vision of the world.

By doing this, you are once again standing back and looking at your life vision. You have described places, events, people— all the tangible aspects of life. By creating another statement that describes the values in your life vision, you are describing the intangible aspects of the life you want to lead. This value statement contains the broad strokes of what drives your life. It identifies basic aspects of what makes you a happy and complete person, and it will direct you to find these intangible values in all the tangible things contained in your life vision.

This is a very important process. It can serve as your point of self-reference, your anchor as you move through the changes that are about to take place in your life. As you systematically move toward transformation in your life, executing the decisions that will bring you there, this value statement will help center you as you tweak and adjust your plans. And it works as a compass to keep you on track once you engage yourself with the myriad of things, events, places and people you are moving toward.

The statement you create should embody the same passion that Martin Luther King, Jr., embodied in his famous "I have a dream" speech. You don't need to be as eloquent, nor will you write at length to illustrate the world in the same dramatic strokes as King, but this vision will contain the essence of what moves you. It should be only three or four sentences long, and you should spend as much time on it as you need to, because this will be the yellowed, tattered card you will still have tucked away in your billfold on the day you die. This is the statement that will guide you for the next fifty years, or however long you have yet to live on this planet. Make it count.

Here's my vision statement, so you can get an idea of what I'm talking about: "I am committed to a world where every part of our lives is a genuine reflection of who we really are; where self-actualization is considered the highest achievement; where people are inspired to pursue their dreams, and where everyone experiences true love." I wrote out my vision statement in a few minutes, but I needed to live with it for a few days, write it and rewrite it until the statement became one that could excite my passion for life, one that could bring me right to the place of total commitment by just reading it. It's a statement that is almost a "shorthand" that prompts my mind to go to the vision I have created. The statement I created is a true description of what I want in my own life, and what I am willing to give in a wholehearted commitment to the world.

It is important to understand why this vision needs to extend beyond your personal interests. If it isn't something that's good for everyone, then you haven't yet distilled it down to its essence.

You will never achieve the results you desire if you hold this vision too close. Values are alive, they are the reality that is impossible to measure or control, and they are present everywhere, all the time.

To serve these values, to acknowledge them as the vitality that drives your vision, is to acknowledge your relatedness to life, to the world, and to everyone in it. This vision is not just for you. You have accepted a mission of bringing these values into life in a way that only you are capable of doing. You have particular ideas and dreams that you will work on to make your life more fulfilling, more exciting and more in line with the life you love. But to believe this can be done without understanding its significance as a part of the whole is to deny the very existence of life itself.

We aren't separate from one another. We have the capacity to make a difference in the world through our own vision and efforts. In your efforts, when you commit to these greater values, you will have the assistance of something much greater than yourself: the invisible force that will pull your vision forward into the reality of the life you desire.

When I did the first exercise of writing out the life I wanted for myself, one of the specific things I saw in that ideal life was to be able to encourage women to live the kind of lives that reflect the powerful, authentic brilliance of their inner selves. Although my personal vision of the world does not go into that kind of detail, it describes the essence of that goal by stating that I am committed to a world where "every part of our lives is a genuine reflection of who we really are" and that "people are inspired to pursue their dreams."

These value statements reflect a life in which I want to be more authentic, but in realizing the universality of those values, I am also committed to helping others live them as well.

When you complete your value statement, and you've lived with it for a while, then you need to bring it to the world. As you've probably noticed, each time you have come to certain realizations throughout this process, I have asked you to share them with others. It can be a very powerful experience to "go public" about your decisions and commitments. As long as you remain private in these decisions, there is something you are holding back; you stay safe, just in case things don't turn out the way you want them to. Don't trade your passion for safety. There is no room for holding back now.

YOUR TOOLKIT

EVERY GOOD SHEBIKER PREPARES WELL BEFORE SHE HEADS out on the road. There's not a lot of room for extra baggage, so she relies mainly on her wits and spirit to survive. For a SheBiker, some of her most important tools aren't in the pack she has tucked away on her bike for motorcycle emergencies. Instead, they are well-developed mental and spiritual tools, habits and attitudes that sharpen her assessment of the world around her, keep her alert and clear-headed, and allow her to be in touch with her divine creativity.

One of the most important tools you can have is a conscious process for making decisions. Rarely do any of us think much about this, but making good decisions allows you to progress toward your vision, and it keeps you aligned with the values you stand for. Decision-making is closely tied to whether you are operating in a reactive mode or a creative mode. If you are still filling your days with to-do lists based on the needs of everyone around you, or if you make decisions based on whether that decision will gain approval from others, you are like a swimmer treading water out in the middle of the ocean, swimming a couple of strokes this way, then turning and swimming a couple of strokes that way. You have no real direction. It's exhausting. You're not making any progress. You have to make progress. There will be time to rest later. The world needs you to participate now.

Here are some questions to ask yourself when you're unclear on which direction to take:

Am I simply choosing from what I think is available to me,
or am I choosing what I really want?

Am I setting conditions on this decision? (I will do this *if* or
when ...)

Am I asking everyone around me to make the decision for me?

Am I playing victim and letting circumstances make the
choice for me?

Am I escalating the issue to the point at which it can be
resolved only one way?

Most of us believe that a decision has to be based on what our options are. While this sounds logical enough, it's a rather limiting way to look at the arena of choice. Instead, begin with the ideal answer and work backward from there. You may find that although such a choice wasn't obvious to you in the beginning, there's really no reason why you couldn't *create* a new choice that is, in fact, doable.

This all sounds rather simplistic, but the truth is, we're all a little like the prisoners from the musical story in the previous chapter: We've gotten used to believing our lives have walls. Consequently, we make decisions that are narrow and self-limiting. But the truth is, the only real freedom we have is the freedom to choose. Once we've exercised the mental stamina to clearly identify the result we want and the commitment is made, we can use creative tension to get to that result. It may have nothing to do with the options around us, but instead be something entirely from our creative imagination.

This is generally called "thinking outside the box." Some people are better at it than others. The best way to get outside the box is to concentrate on the end result from the beginning. Don't forget, you've got a brilliant mind as well as divine insight that's available to you 24/7, so if you can be clear about what you want to create, you're perfectly capable of finding the way to get there.

Women tend to be process-oriented. It's the way we're hard-wired. But that doesn't mean we have to let it rule our lives. It just means we are good at defining the "how" in a situation. But getting to the how before you understand what you're after is a very roundabout way of moving through life. In fact, it's nearly impossible to create any sort of direction when you don't know your destination.

Remember the story about my girlfriend who wanted a better job and decided she needed to go back to school to get it? Not only did she have difficulty seeing herself as already qualified, she also hastily came to the "how" of that goal before she really settled on the result. We usually think that's a prudent way to get moving. It certainly beats just sitting around thinking about things for weeks on end. But most women could stand to exercise a little more patience about thinking things through before they launch out on another project.

I have another friend who wanted to move out of her house. Her kids were gone, and the house was too big. She immediately called her realtor and started looking at other homes. This wasn't painful—she's the kind of person who loves to tour other people's houses. The problem was, she really didn't stop to think through what she was after, and as the weeks and then months passed, she was no closer to her goal of finding another place to live. When she finally did stop to define the result she wanted to achieve, she realized she wanted to move back to her hometown. She would never have stumbled on that conclusion by touring more houses.

Define your result before you consider the how. Then let creative tension do its magic. This is an important consideration, because the world isn't the same one we grew up in. Critical situations in our world have accelerated over the last century to near-breakneck speed. We don't have the luxury of half-heartedly making decisions anymore. They all have to count.

Not only do they have to count, but if you consider some of the things we have to overcome—poverty, violence, starvation, prejudice—trying to figure these things out by ourselves can be overwhelming and leave us apathetic, which is where most of the world is today. We don't think we can make things better. We don't know how. But knowing how is not the point. We must first commit to a particular result, and then let divine insight guide us there. If we are not wedded to a particular process, we will more easily cooperate with available resources to achieve the results we need.

So as you consider decisions, don't limit yourself to what you see in front of you. Envision the result you want, and then commit to making it happen. Everything else will follow.

Once you've made your decisions, realize that there is a hierarchy of primary choices and secondary choices that lead you to your goal. *Primary* choices have a broader result to them. If I decide I want to ride a motorcycle, then I embody that decision and become a Biker. The primary choice that follows from that is to get a motorcycle. Another primary choice is to keep my bike in good condition so I can ride safely.

A *secondary* or supporting choice would be to replace my tires when they wear out. Just choosing to replace my tires doesn't have nearly the sweeping result that choosing to keep my bike in good condition has—it's *part of* that broader decision to maintain my bike well. Conversely, keeping my bike in good condition doesn't encompass all the things that make me a Biker.

When you find yourself struggling with a decision that has become confusing, you may be mixing up primary choices with secondary choices. A woman I know wanted to become a professional photographer. One of her primary choices was to develop an advisory board of people who could influence her career. However, before she chose the advisory board, she found herself spending a lot of time trying to figure out whether she should put up a website for these people so they could see her work, or prepare prints to mail out to them.

She placed secondary decisions before primary decisions, and her plans got muddied. If she had first identified the people who would be on her advisory board—her primary decision—then all she would have had to do is ask them how they'd prefer to receive the images, and her secondary decision would have practically been made for her. When decisions are made in hierarchical order, they tend to flow more smoothly.

This may seem a little tedious, but I promise you, understanding the hierarchy of decisions and defining your result before you start mapping out your process are two tools that will help smooth the ride toward your destination.

Once you've made some important decisions, you'll begin to move toward your goal through a creative process that has a beginning, a middle and an end. A tool in your SheBiker kit that will help you is an awareness of these different phases.

The first phase is the *germination*. This is the really fun phase where you're excited about your new idea and you've got lots of energy to give to it. The idea takes up a lot of your thinking time, and moving forward is enjoyable and somewhat effortless. To use the most obvious analogy, this would be conception, or more specifically, the act of lovemaking, where the passion and life forces come together to make something new. Exciting though it is, it doesn't last, and we're off to the next phase.

The next phase is *assimilation*. It takes place in a quiet way, and a lot of the development that goes on isn't easy to follow. It's kind of like being pregnant, except that with a creative idea, you don't have the confidence that nature is moving forward with or without you. But just like pregnancy, there's not a lot you can do to make things go faster than they organically want to go. The creative process isn't something you can piece together so it doesn't make you anxious or so that it pleases everyone around you. Trying to control the process limits the possibilities of what can happen.

While you're exercising patience, also be aware of new opportunities in the moment. You've done your planning and organizing to achieve results, but you would also do well to stay open to new input. These are the little, correcting decisions that make your original plans more effective in the face of new information. As long as you stay clear on what you want for your results, you won't get thrown off course even as you make small changes in your original plans.

The way you define what you are experiencing is a crucial part of the assimilation process. People often give up too soon, when in fact their actions are very effective but haven't yet shown results. Edison had an idea about how to make a light bulb. He tried almost a hundred times and failed. If he had seen each of these attempts as the end result of his efforts, he might have given up. Instead, as he described it, he discovered ninety-nine ways *not* to build a light bulb.

If you feel you are standing still or even going backward when you are working toward a result, chances are you are in the midst of the quiet of assimilation. There may not be a problem, but you can certainly take the opportunity to reassess the status of the results you're creating. Try this exercise to see if you need to do something more at this time or if you're just being impatient:

1. Take the time to get a new "reading" on your current reality.
2. Revisit the results you wish to create.
3. Recommit yourself to the choices that will lead you to those results.
4. Change the focus of your attention—literally distract yourself with something else.
5. Get out of the way. Let creative tension do its thing in creating the most effective and direct route from where you are to where you want to be.

The next phase is *completion,* and obviously, the analogy is the birth of a child. I find this analogy interesting, because if you've ever given birth, you know there are a few terrifying moments when you realize the enormity of what you've done and that there's no going back. Of course, the vast majority of us stop being terrified because we fall so in love with our offspring, but other results we create don't always look so adorable. Some results don't look anything like we thought they would, and we stop just short of achieving our goal because, well, things are going to change now, and wouldn't it just be easier to slide back to the familiar?

The completion phase can be difficult for other reasons, too. As badly as you want certain results in your life, you may be uncomfortable with success. It may mean you're showing up on the radar screen for the first time. You're no longer the demure little thing who doesn't call attention to herself; now you're out there being uppity, thinking you have power. Here come the rotten tomatoes.

All of these things occur to women who have been raised not to rock the boat, to let the boyfriend win the card game, to be seen and not heard, to be ladylike and not boisterous, yada yada yada. That training needs to be wiped clean from our life perspective. This is no time to be reserved. There are millions and millions of people in the world right now who are struggling to stay alive because they don't have enough to eat. There are men and women and their precious children who don't have adequate access to the health care they need, including a lot of hardworking people right here in the United States. There are atrocities happening to defenseless people that I can't even think about without falling into a deep funk because they're so creepy and outrageous. There is much to do right in our own communities to bring about equal opportunity for everyone.

Those issues are the tip of the iceberg. Your passion could very well be about something entirely different. As a matter of fact, you may be the only person who really cares about your issue. But you may be the person who turns the tide.

We have to fine-tune our abilities to become effective change-makers. We have no choice. We're about to leave this planet, sooner than any of us are ready for, and when we do, we will have either contributed or missed our chance to give something back to a beautiful place that once gave us life.

Progress. Don't leave home without it.

THE FLOW OF THE JOURNEY

WHEN I WAS GROWING UP, I HEARD IN CHURCH THE STORY OF Paul of Tarsus. Paul was a first-century persecutor of Christians, and he was a terror. One day, while walking down the road to Damascus to wreak more havoc on the Christians, he was blinded by a heavenly light, and he heard the voice of Jesus. "Paul, Paul," the voice from heaven said, "why do you persecute me?" It was a moment of salvation for a man full of judgment and hate, and the light of Jesus' love streaming forth from heaven made him do a 180. From that moment on, he became one of Christianity's staunchest advocates.

I always envied Paul. There could be no doubt in his mind what he was supposed to be doing with his life. Not that life was easy for him; he got kicked out of a lot of places and he worked hard, often with few results, but he had an agenda that had the holy stamp of approval.

Do you remember my fantasy about the Queen SheBiker? Indulge me please, there's more. In my fantasy, once the Queen resolves my money issues, transforms my children into compliant family members, and generally takes care of all my material needs, she will hand me an embossed leather dossier that contains a neatly defined agenda for my life. This agenda will tell me exactly what I need to do, list the activities that will best utilize my talents, and give me goals and timelines to follow.

That would be ideal, wouldn't it? Because it isn't easy to know what we're supposed to be doing with our lives. Even if we think we *might* know what we're supposed to be doing, once we've started down the road to our goals, their effectiveness and appropriateness are rarely possible to verify. Most of us will never have the confirmation Paul experienced of his life's mission. No matter how fervently we may be asking to receive enlightenment, and no matter how completely we'd dedicate ourselves if the task were assigned to us from On High, chances are we'll never really know if we're doing the right thing.

Most of us are intelligent enough to interpret our everyday experiences, and we develop wisdom, insight and meaning from those experiences. But rarely do we pay enough attention to develop the kind of conviction that makes us confident about our choices. Our tendency to avoid the mental effort of thinking anything through means a lot of us put our understanding of life's purpose somewhere between our half-hearted efforts to floss on a regular basis and getting our taxes done before the last minute. Sure, it's something we should engage in so we have a clearer sense of where we're going. But who has the time to develop that kind of insight? Followed closely by, what's in it for me?

Becoming aware of divine insight, of that still, small voice within you, is an essential part of sanity and of growing your awareness outside of the Holy Trinity of Me, Myself and I. Sorting out the important stuff and learning to interpret life's experiences in a meaningful way help you understand what choices will make you the happiest, most fulfilled person you can be. A good take on reality is even more important in how it can give you a sense of your place in the scheme of things and of your relation to the big picture. The more you understand how your actions affect the world around you, the wiser you will become, and the more prepared you will be as an agent of real change on the Biker Planet.

If we are to become wiser in our thinking, our living and our relations with one another, we need to look to love. Because love is the real guide to insight. Love lets us look at reality through God's eyes, to see things for the good of everyone involved without self-interest or unspoken needs. Not only does it give us the most objective outlook, but it contains within it the most essential force—the life force. It inspires us to be more creative and constructive. In the final analysis, love is the most authentic value of all.

Few of us understand what love really is. True love is the source of the qualities that are at the core of our being, at the core of every person. So it's more than an emotion, it is a *reality*. This reality manifests itself as courage, loyalty, tenderness and forgiveness, to name a few of the values it creates. Although its presence is intangible, it is the most powerful aspect of our humanity. Love is responsible for life itself, because it chooses *progress*. Love is imbued with a life force that invariably overcomes the most disgusting forms of evil. Love gives us our true power.

Love connects us to something greater than ourselves. It's important to have that expansion of self, because it helps us understand that we're all connected to each other. When we see each other as "other," we can't transcend our disgust with our current situation here on Earth. It's only when we feel the relatedness that we feel compelled to help one another. But it's not just an emotion that connects us. Love is so much more than an emotion. It is a divine reality. And the more we experience it, the more we get to know God, because God is love.

Getting to know God and becoming more real through the expression of love, lived through your highest values, is something you have to do for yourself. It has to be taken out of the mental arena and expressed through your actions in order to make it real on an individual basis. It also has to be something you come to on your own, not because you're told to do it. You can't just sit there in a pew on Sunday morning and nod in approval—it has to be lived. It would be unwise to ignore those who are truly gifted and who can teach us a lot about spirituality. But ultimately, it's our own ability to create insight in the very moment it's needed that will move the planet forward.

Our sense of spirituality is invariably linked with this understanding of love as a divine reality, and women have been busy redefining that spirituality in the last fifty years. We need to be authentic to be powerful in every regard, and it certainly includes the way we connect to our understanding of the Divine. But sometimes our reaction to what we want to get away from in religion is to swing the pendulum way over to the left, and there has been plenty of swinging going on in women's exploration for a true spiritual home.

Women have been searching in earnest over the last few decades for a way to define their spirituality. Before we really thought through all the possibilities to construct a framework that represents a beautiful, elegant concept of spirituality—something progressive and thoughtful—many women adopted a religious symbolism they surmised must be true because, they were told, it's so old. In much the same way that religionists often sit there in their pews and just drink in whatever they're told from the pulpit, many women drank in the idea that a maternal utopia once existed, where the feminine Goddess ruled. It sounds like a good alternative to what we don't want from organized religion, but it may in fact be just another third-party authority in disguise.

The point is not to replace the male-dominated belief systems, rituals, incense, Eucharist, yada yada yada, with kitsch of our own choosing. The point is to become lean, strong SheBikers and to access a pure connection that comes straight from the Source, appropriate to the moment and ever so true-north. We can't become a viable conduit for the will of Divine Grace on this screwed-up planet if we have to detour through a maze of New Age paraphernalia that still says: "I'm not capable of receiving this information directly; I need this token and that taliswoman to intervene on my not-quite-sufficient behalf."

We have within us the purest connection to the most incredible wisdom in all of reality. We have an actual spark of Divinity connecting the lowest animal-origin mortal (that would be us) with the highest Divine Creatress (that would be Her), and no amount of kitsch is going to make you more eligible for that direct connection. Perhaps some form of spiritual ritual can help you focus in on divine insight, but I invite you to consider that it is often just another distraction from what you can do for yourself, which is:

Get really clear about the values that turn you on.
Commit to bringing those values into the world through a
    noble purpose.
Make choices that *always* stay true to your commitment.
Be courageous in accepting the opportunities that come
    your way.
Remain conscious of how life is a partnership between you
    and the Divine.
Stay grateful.
Don't confuse control with order.
Realize that chaos comes before change.
Trust God to take care of your soul.
Tap into love to take care of the rest.

Once you get into the "flow" of such an attitude, your life becomes exciting, fresh and meaningful, beyond the importance or weight that extra stuff can add to your identity. Look at you! You're awesome! Stripped naked and shivering in the cold, you've got more going for you than any feng shui wind chime or sage stick could add to the mix. You're the real thing, and you are exactly complete just as you are, as long as you have another breath to breathe and a fist to clench in the determination necessary to bring this ball of mud back into the light of sanity.

Instead of surrounding ourselves with the *symbols* of empowerment, let's just go ahead and empower ourselves outright. Oh, why not. Let's use those fabulous minds of ours. The divine will for this planet is the most reasonable, sane, loving path we can imagine. It's not magical or mysterious; it's exactly what we would do if we were Queen. Once we've got the ideal front and center in our minds, it's time to get out there and make it happen.

The Road Ahead

CONTACT IS A MOVIE BASED ON THE BEST-SELLING BOOK BY Carl Sagan. It's a story about the first contact made by another planet with the people on our planet, prompted by popular radio and television broadcasts received as transmitted waves that traveled away from the Earth.

The movie opens with the camera moving across the surface of the planet, "listening" to the accumulating cacophony of voices and music being broadcast. Then the camera lifts the viewer up and away from the Earth's surface, looking backward at the Earth as it diminishes in size, while we listen to everything from an Adolf Hitler speech to the *I Love Lucy* show—long-ago broadcasts traveling like a time machine through space. Moving beyond stars and galaxies, we're eventually so far away from Earth that all sound fades and the starry space becomes silent.

The first time I saw that scene, I considered how such a view, in the rearview mirror as it were, might be similar to leaving the planet as a traveler. It made me think about what it will feel like someday when we're no longer citizens of this planet. The tremendous distances the movie portrayed between our sun and the other stars in the cosmos gave me pause—we don't know if we're ever coming back here once we leave this planet, and we're surely never going to live this particular life again. This is very possibly the last chance we'll ever have to help this confused, bewildered, beautiful place.

What will we leave behind as a gift to this world? What part of us will continue as a legacy in the culture of this planet?

Can you imagine a conversation we might have with another

traveler 300 years from now, when they find out we were born on the Biker Planet? "Wow," they'll exclaim, "that must have been some experience! I've heard about that place. What was life like there?" Unless we consciously change how we interact with life, most of us will likely rattle off a litany of absolutely meaningless trifles with which we were so preoccupied that, in retrospect, we might as well not have been born at all.

What are we waiting for? I don't know about you, but my life gets more complicated as I grow older. If I'm waiting for some ideal moment to start getting serious about dedicating more of my time and effort to making this a better place, I'm fairly certain I've missed my chance. I think that window of opportunity briefly appeared somewhere around my fifth birthday.

We have two reasons for being here, just as we have two arenas of experience. One is our relationship with that "oneness" we feel inside, our divine center; the other is our life in relation to other people, the planet and the universe. We use the challenges and experiences we have here to develop as individuals, to grow closer to the divine potential, to become more of who we really are.

Trying to be someone we're not is probably the most ridiculous time-waster we'll manage to have in the eternity of our lifetime. How silly is the life most of us lead, spending our brain power trying to please others, look like others, and think like others. Ultimately, we'll find that the most direct path to personal evolution is in getting really good at being who we are.

Giving something back to the planet is a reaction we should be having to the joy of becoming evolved individuals and connecting to divine inspiration. But since so few of us are in that joyful connection, the planet is a little behind on its quota of humans being wonderful to each other. It's hard to be kind to others when you're in pain yourself. But that's our challenge, isn't it? And as most of us have experienced, it's the only answer to transcending the pain. In some sort of Catch-22, we can't experience the fullness of what it is to be ourselves until we're thinking of others. It's a circle back to God. God gives love to us, and we give it to and receive it from others. God experiences the love from inside both the giver and the recipient, and it goes round and round in a delicious circle.

It works the way a light bulb works: Forming the connecting conduit between the two filaments of wire inside the bulb makes the current flow. One filament won't do the job. There has to be an energy flow between the two of them before there's any light. Our duty is actually our greatest privilege: to take the building blocks of imperfection and, in concert with divine inspiration, allow the flow of divine love to reach out to other people through our decisions and actions, giving light to this very dark planet.

We are just beginning to understand this universe we live in, and we're just beginning to actualize the persons we will someday complete. Socially, it's not just our neighborhood or even our planet that we have an impact on as we evolve—we are part of a vast universe teeming with life, and our ability to make a difference extends far beyond our lives here. Thinking globally is a good way to frame our experience, but thinking cosmically is really our destiny. One aspect of loving service has to do with the way it affects our planet, but as we share the experience of loving with that divine spark in our minds, we affect the entire cosmic soul. In an interesting circular motion, not only are we contributing to the betterment of our planet—we are also contributing to the universe age in which we are evolving.

Whether we see things in an extended view or as limited to a lifetime on this planet, we are moved to love and to act when we experience pain or suffering or watch it occur to others. Sometimes it feels overwhelming instead of inspiring, though. We feel apathy instead of empathy when we view the enormous problems our planet faces. We have so much to do just to keep our own lives going, and we often don't know where to begin with one little life and all these really big problems.

But the truth of it is, it takes more energy to constantly be compromising what we know is right than it does to try to create change. It's harder to sit and stew in righteous indignation than it is to spend time finding and joining a kindred group of people, in our hometowns or on the Internet, who are in forward motion working toward something that matters to us. It takes more energy to always be pushing the anger down than it does to use our creative minds to start in the place where we find ourselves and make a difference, even if it's only for one other person.

As women, we're often too willing to believe that someone else knows more than we do; that any words we speak in protest will be shot down as naïve and simplistic; that we're just being Pollyanna-ish in thinking something should be better than it is. In Western culture, there's a weird silence that overtakes the pure of heart when the cynical, so-called sophisticate is mouthing off and telling us we should just sit back and allow the hilarity of it all to sink in.

Cynicism is a brutal sophistry and one of the creepiest things on this planet. It is fear, cloaked in denial. It's also self-fulfilling. How can things get any better if we don't do anything to make them so? Demanding that things get better is hardly being naïve. It's the most courageous thing you can do, and it's a necessary action if we want our children and our children's children to have a better place to live. If we work hard to make things better, the least we can do is succeed in keeping things from getting any worse.

You know a lot more than you think you do. Just as we all share the same values, we also share many of the same problems. Your experiences with the struggles of life are probably very similar to the struggles of a lot of other people on the planet. That means you are just as capable as the next person of finding solutions—or better yet, a more compelling vision of a better way.

Why should we even try? Do things really get any better? Do people ever acquire more capacity to overcome evil? Yes, they do, they have, and they will. It's imperative that we give our contribution to this slow but sure evolution. The universe is very much like a vast university in which all of life everywhere is one big learning experience. That's the goal—experience. The worlds of time and space revolve around the eternal home of God, and the destiny of every one of Her trillions of children is to make their way home to Paradise, experiencing and evolving into amazing spiritual beings, sharing time and space with the Spirit within them every step of the way.

If progress is the watchword of the universe, then we must all be participating in an enormous undertaking to move finite reality closer to perfection. Every time we overcome evil with love, even if it's only in our own minds, we are bringing this universal reality a little closer to its ultimate destiny. Even as we struggle for social equity and better conditions for our brothers and sisters in this life on this planet, there is an eternal purpose for that struggle as well. The world needs to be made a better place, but the experience we have in the process is also a valuable contribution, because the mind we share with God is also the mind that evolves the cosmos, and that also affects this planet.

Things are a little tougher for us here on the crazy Biker Planet than on a more normal home sphere. As I've said before, you don't have to believe anything about whether there are other planets or whether they're better off than we are to know, in your gut, that things should be better than they are. There is a job to do; we're the ones who have to do it, and we have to do it now.

We need to plan and prepare our minds for this incredible challenge. We have to find the perspective to keep our vision clear and the sustenance to keep our countenance strong. We each need to develop a conceptual framework that fits our own perspective on life, so we can understand reality and work with it. In other words, we need to consciously develop a "life view" that serves us.

We develop this life view by identifying the values we care about and allowing them to guide us. If you've done the exercises earlier in this book, then you have a value statement that says "This is what I stand for. This is what I'm about and I'm going to commit myself to bringing these values into the world in a bigger way than the way they're here right now."

I'm not telling you something you don't already know, but I hope that by having this "conversation" with me in your mind, you'll be motivated to push a little harder to put that together. It's like cleaning out a closet: you know it's a good idea, but there are always so many other things to do. Well, our minds are full of things that need to be given away or taken out to the curb for pickup. We need to lighten the distractions and get mentally fit and focused so we can be effective in creating change here. Neither wishful thinking nor hoping the right situation will present itself is an effective way to transform yourself or others. We're SheBikers, and we must develop persistence to do and be what we think is right. We're creating, not responding. It requires conscious effort, but it's necessary and exhilarating.

I feel honored that I have this opportunity to applaud your efforts—the spirit of strength in women is going to transform this world in the next few hundred years. It is so important that we are blazing a path of new identity for the girls and women who come after us, just as the women who came before us have inspired us. Where we stand now in this period of opportunity is the culmination of the hard work, determination and phenomenal courage of women who have lived here for thousands of years.

As we come into our power, we won't take that power lightly; we know such power can change the quality of life for others. We care about how others suffer, because suffering has been our legacy. It's not the only thing we've known, but we do know it well.

As a gender, and as individuals, we need to understand that the time has come to use our power. The world doesn't have to give it to us; it is ours already. We access it by realizing that we are a part of something much greater than ourselves. Love is the flow we tap into for power.

If you're thinking that love has weakened you, then you're not really thinking about love. The biggest difference between love and being a doormat is how a woman regards herself. If you know that you deserve every bit as much respect as you are willing to give others, then you are in the context of true love. If you think people have to step all over you before you really get a chance to show love, then you're using the wrong word to describe what you're putting yourself through.

Our power is in love, because love is the greatest reality in the universe. It provides the clearest insight, gives us the most poise and courage, and helps us lead lives that are balanced and real. It removes defiance and anger, which cloud the real purpose and direction of creative change. It allows you to tap into something that witnesses to your soul that you are a child of an infinite, loving deity. Such a realization gives you the self-respect and courage to get out in the world and change things. Love also provides you with a vision of life that can replace the cultural malaise and chaos the world experiences now.

Once you're clear on your values, find a purpose that serves the values that inspire you. Own that purpose in how you see yourself—in your identity. Do you harbor secret dreams you don't think you have a right to bring into the world? You do have to bring them into the world, my dear Sister. They are the reflection of your greatness, and you know deep down inside that you need to be playing a bigger game than you are right now. Chances are you're leading less of a life than you're capable of leading. We need you out in the world in the fullness of your talents and gifts. When you know what your purpose is, you'll have to take a leap of faith and commit to making it happen. If it fails, well, it won't be the first time you've had to back up and try again. Your purpose is something only you can know for sure, and although you can benefit from the wise opinions of others, you're going to have to make the commitment to making it happen yourself.

Life goes on for eons. As we become wiser and older, we will become more and more brilliant beings. Let the theologians argue about where all that takes place—if you want my opinion, read *The Urantia Book*, which has the most detailed description of life after death of any document on the planet. The point is, we've barely begun our eternal journey, and although we can certainly wait until we're further along in our universe careers before we drop the deer-in-the-headlights stupor, why not get after it now and make a difference here? I have a very strong feeling that this particular planet needs us more than any other place we'll ever be.

The good news is, we're not alone. There are many people in the world who are helping this planet. They are everywhere. And with the Internet, it is easier and easier to connect to like-minded individuals. We do have the ability to make a difference, and we don't have to do it by ourselves.

For example, at the time of this writing, I get one to five email newsletters and action alerts every day from organizations working at change. I've signed up for these emails because they make it incredibly easy for me to write to my senator to tell him how I want him to vote on a particular bill, or to send a quick twenty-five dollars to an organization that needs help funding something I believe in, or to read what some of the brightest people have to say about issues that interest me.

The more knowledgeable I am about issues I believe in, the better I know how to vote, and the more capable I am of communicating a personal vision of what I think needs to happen to make the world a better place. The more familiar I am with the issues that move me, the better I can prioritize how I want to spend my time working for change. And it's all so easy; in most cases, information is no longer a barrier for world change.

But intellectual assent to a cause does nothing unless it moves your heart. Don't sign on to a cause because you think you should or it's a popular place to be. Let it move you. You'll be no good to it if you don't make yourself vulnerable to what's taking place. It's tough, I know, to feel the pain. Sometimes I tell God that I can't take any more exposure to what's wrong with this planet. I have the audacity to wonder if She really knows what it's like to feel this way. But then I remind myself that I'm an infant in my understanding of reality. And sometimes I even allow myself to believe that it may just be that things are getting better.

Love is the greatest reality in the universe. Every time we push everyday reality a little closer to the direction of love, we're taking the imperfection of time and space and working out a little more of how love overcomes evil. It doesn't always happen that way, but even in our planet's history, we can see how things turn out for the good in the longer view. It's still scary-crazy down here, but it's far from being hopeless. Who is to say that your episode with overcoming something painful won't be the time the universe finally settles how love triumphs over chaos for that issue? Experience is the essential element for evolution. We can't just hypothesize our way into perfection.

We are in the middle of a long evolutionary struggle, and love is proving time and again how much God and people need each other. Our free will decisions get us—and others—into so much trouble that it's truly a miracle that love can rescue us from our own arrogance and stupidity, but it does. There will come a time, and we'll be there to witness it somewhere in the universe, where the devotion of a Divine Parent and the persistence of Her children will come together in infinite unity. As finite experience evolves to perfection, another episode of reality will complete itself full circle. And we get to come along for the ride.

Spirit Rules. Don't ever doubt it. As disgusting as this planet can be, we are moving forward in the right direction. Our planet is part of a friendly, organized universe. When our mind's eye gives us our first glimpse of the cosmos that is our home, it's like the lid is lifted off the world, and we understand that we belong to the universe and it belongs to us.

It would be sheer arrogance to deny that the universe is inhabited. It is expanding and refining as it evolves toward the culmination of a master plan that has been going on for a very long time.

The difficulty we have with thinking about all of this, with envisioning a new cosmic perspective, is that we often try to make such expanding thoughts fit into our current frame of reference. We have no planetary legacy that everyone agrees on. We all have bits and pieces; some of it is curiously parallel, but there are no surviving cultures that act as a repository for our planet's history or give us insight into how we fit into the scheme of the cosmos around us. Religion's portrayal of history is practically a moving target, depending on what century and what religion you're in.

Are we really in the middle of a tug-of-war between good and evil? It can be hard to imagine that goodness has the upper hand in our world. It can be very difficult to believe that God can love us and at the same time allow us to endure some of the horrible things that happen on this planet. The only way we can allow atrocities to be considered in the same thought as a loving benevolent Deity is not through denial, but through understanding.

In the same way that we all make more sense of our lives as we view them in longer time units, we can rectify the seemingly unrectifiable aspects of reality by expanding our viewpoint to a cosmic breadth. Our lives include a time frame for our future that will stretch out through eons and light years, allowing us to process and use every moment of our existence to gain wisdom and pass on the lessons from all of our struggles. We already do that, even with nothing more than a few years of expanded insight.

Many years ago, my then-husband's business went bankrupt. It was awful. My husband suffered intense feelings of failure and shame. People avoided us as if we had leprosy. Some of the shareholders in the company who used to be our friends literally cornered my husband in a public place, threatening to sue him as if, in some twisted plot, the management had taken the company down on purpose. The bank was coming after our house. We were selling everything that had any value in an attempt to pay our bills, and the money from the sales was ridiculously insufficient for the enormity of our problems.

A friend of mine called me one day when all this was going on and suggested we meet for coffee. She was an adult trust-fund kid who had had the ride of her life through her twenties with millions of dollars that had become hers through the wealth of a family trust—that is, before her accountant embezzled all her money and left her penniless. She had never worked a day in her life up until then, and it took her another ten years to figure out how to make a decent living. In many ways, she had already been through what we were going through.

"Carol," she said over coffee, "I know you think this is your life. You think you're on some downward slide into hell and you're never going to recover. But all of this will be behind you in a year or two. Things *will* feel normal again." I clung to that promise over the next few years. I believed her, because she had the understanding that comes from having gone through it. And you know what? She was right. We did get through it.

These are the times in life when we present ourselves to each other without pretense; when we're facing each other honestly as growing, imperfect human beings. The sharing of our experiences of pain and our struggles to overcome our fears are some of the most meaningful ways we connect with one another. People who go through Twelve Step programs or other support groups experience the same realness of connection; there is nothing more powerful than knowing you've been to Hell and back and lived to tell the tale.

SheBikers are being called to own this connection with our sisters and brothers. We need to have the courage to believe that the commonality of our experience is our most powerful bond and also our clearest path for service to others. Hard times testify to the fact that this is not an easy planet to live on. The good news is, in those moments of pain, we receive our greatest gift: the giving and receiving of true love, both from each other, and from the Source.

As we progress down this very rocky road, we still have access to the most real of all assistance—a part of divinity that indwells each of our minds. It's difficult to prove the existence of such divine guidance unless you step back and take an extended look at the way spirit prevails in this barbaric world, and then its presence is undeniable. No matter what has happened or will happen to us because we start our universe careers on this planet, we have a direct link to the very source and center of all things.

Nothing like our planet has ever existed before. Not in this neck of the universe, anyway. So we don't really know what the future brings. But one thing is certain. Although most of the people on this planet willfully ignore the most exquisite of internal mentors, enough suggestions get through to keep us moving forward. The future of this planet is secured by the rugged determination of an amazing population of Biker-esque inhabitants, the loving care of an indwelling divine presence, and the overcare of a host of celestial beings dedicated to respecting the sovereignty of our free will.

We all have an exciting mission in front of us. We can get really clear about what we believe in, and then be courageous about "being" that belief. We can walk this planet in the full knowledge that we have every right, every talent, and every insight into what we need to do and become to make this world a better place. Once you own that perspective, you can't go back to being a victim, or being apathetic, or embracing any of the other survival strategies we adopt when we think we can't do something. Yes, we can. Yes, we will.

So what's your gift to the planet, dear Sister? Before you start thinking about what you can "do," let me answer the question from my perspective of who you "are," looking back at your beautiful face from these pages we've just shared together.

You are an accomplishment of divine proportions. You have a deep, deep reservoir of greatness that can either remain dormant or come alive to serve the planet and give your consciousness an exhilarating ride in a very short life on a very stormy planet. You know what I'm talking about. You live with the secret of your greatness every day.

The fact that you may have been hurt before when you've opened your heart and reached for your dreams just means that you need to rely on God for support for opening it again, because that's what you're being called to do. Your heart is the portal to your power. Love is the essence of what gives you your vision, helping you see the end from the beginning. Love keeps your gaze on the horizon while it makes you so committed to being a powerful loving woman that your mind will find a way to accomplish your dreams.

You are a unique, brilliant, creative woman. You don't need to assess your worth by the comments and signals from the world around you; you know who you are, and it's time you trusted that gut feeling. God has placed certain perspectives, talents and skills in your personality that are a unique combination, and your mission is to develop those assets so you can join in the thrilling experience of loving this world back into a saving grace.

Don't wait another minute to commit to being as much that person on the outside as you are on the inside. Actualizing your authentic self lifts the veil and takes you to a place from which you can never go back, no matter how many times you lack the faith to admit it. My only regret is that I may not get to hear your story, because I know it's going to be a good one. We'll just have to plan on having lattes at some cosmic café later down the line. In the meantime, stand up and be counted, because you're the one and the time is now. SheBiker, start your engine!

FORMING A KICK START READERS' DISCUSSION GROUP

BEING SEEN AND HEARD AS YOU EXPRESS YOUR TRUTHS, AND being supported as you come clean about your own fears, can be a liberating and growing experience. Giving voice to your dreams and hopes in an atmosphere where others are committed to similar values will support you in moving forward in your life. I've included questions here that are meant not only to help you review and process the information in this book, but to take *Kick Start* into a community of readers for discussion and insight.

I invite you to consider including men in this discussion group. Part of the work that needs to be done is helping men understand us better, and also creating respectful opportunities for us to understand them as well.

ORGANIZING THE GROUP

1. Start by committing to being the driving force of such a group. It will involve only a couple of hours a week for the first month, until the momentum gets going. Every group needs a go-to person, and that person should probably be you. If you've got a phone and access to email, then you're set. This responsibility can be passed around once things are established.

2. Pick a date and a time, perhaps two or three weeks from now. Commit to it. (Make your time realistic for getting there after work.) Call your best friend, or better yet, three friends, and brainstorm with them about two dozen or so friends who

might be interested in attending a group. Depending on the size of your living room, you will have better discussions with no more than six or eight people. If the group gets too big, you can always split it in two.

3. Before you contact any of your candidates, think about why you want to start a discussion group. If you need to, write it down. I have a tendency to ramble, so I always make notes, or else I would take fifteen minutes to say something that can be said in five. Here are a couple of examples of what someone might say to introduce the idea: "The other day at work, someone got a birthday cake for one of our coworkers. We all went into the kitchen, and the women immediately started getting everything together and cutting the cake and serving it, while the men stood around and talked and waited to get their piece of cake. It was frustrating how the women automatically started doing all the grunt work, and I realized that we were just as guilty about it as the men were. I want to start 'owning' the responsibility of changing stereotypical roles, most especially in myself, and I think this book might help me explore how I can promote those changes in my life. I thought you might be interested in looking at that, too, as well as other issues about how women limit themselves, and how we can do a better job at asking for what we want."

Or this: "I want to get involved in improving how women are treated by society, such as fighting against legislation that takes away the rights of women making decisions regarding their own bodies, or human rights issues around the world where women frequently have no protection against violence in civil wars. I know there's a lot I could be doing here in our hometown. I don't have much money to give to charity, and I don't have all the time in the world, so I'd like to get clear about what it is that really moves me the most. But to do that, I need to explore the issues. I think this book would help spark that discussion, and I thought your voice would be a great addition to such a discussion."

4. You could email your candidates, but it would actually be better to call them first. The reason you want to talk directly to them is that you need to connect on an emotional level with the importance of exploring these issues. Otherwise, it's just another appointment they have to keep. People need to be reminded why these things matter.

5. One week before the first meeting, email a reminder to everyone who said they were interested in coming. If they don't have email, skip this and add the info to your reminder phone call. Ask them to reply with a commitment as to whether they intend to be there. Tell them when the meeting will start and when it will end. If needed, include a link to MapQuest (*www.mapquest.com*) in your email to show the location of your home. For the first meeting, suggest that everyone read the introduction and chapter 1 and write answers to the questions for that section, or at least look them over in advance and give them some thought.

I've done this a lot, and I have always had better turnout when I call a couple of days before the first group meeting and remind people again. I know it's easier to do it during the day when you know you're going to get voicemail, but you'll have better results if you get a live person. Make it brief.

Keeping the Group Effective

These discussion groups can turn into the most meaningful evenings of your everyday life. You want to keep them fun and spontaneous, but a little planning ahead will get everyone on the same page and avoid misunderstandings later.

Logistics

❖ Try rotating the location. It's fun to go to and host these meetings in different places. If you don't make those choices before the end of the evening ("Okay, who wants to host the next meeting?"), then be sure someone in the group communicates the place to others and is readily available to respond to queries about the location.

❖ Begin and end when you say you will. Ideally, a meeting time should be established and held to over a long period. This way it will become generally known that your group meets, for example, on Monday nights. This will make it easier for people who can't come to every meeting to remember when the meetings are held.

❖ Always have a beverage or water available during the meeting. Dessert is a wonderful ritual when it comes to home meetings. People love the celebratory symbol of dessert—it says "This is a special time." After all, they made the effort to join you. Preparing something special communicates how honored you are to have them in your home. Women who have issues around eating may prefer fruit or nuts to the traditional dessert you're serving. You know your friends. Prepare accordingly.

Discussion Rules

One of the best ways to keep group discussion healthy is to set discussion rules in advance. You might want to craft an agreement within the group to keep discussion "clean," confidential, and on track. Have the rules read and agreed upon by the group before each meeting.

❖ Confidentiality is a big dang deal in these meetings. If the members of your group can't feel safe here, they won't have nearly the experience of sharing and learning that they could have. This is an opportunity to practice living in integrity.

The statement of rules could include that two people in the group wouldn't be acting in integrity if they discussed, outside the group, what a third member said. It might include that no one, but no one, talks about what happens to the others at the meetings, even with significant others. If your significant other asks you what happened at the meeting, you say what happened to you, but not the others.

❖ Own your own judgments—if it's not a fact, it's your opinion. Share it as such. "In my judgment" is a good phrase for everyone to learn.

❖ Members of the group should never offer advice to each other unless they've been given permission to do so. Encourage each other to be honest about whether or not you're in the mood for advice.

❖ Encourage each other not to feel any of you have to defend your position when someone offers another point of view. Hearing lots of points of view is what group interaction is all about.

❖ You might consider using a nondistracting object to indicate who has the floor for speaking; pass it in turn to each person who wants to speak, so everyone doesn't try to speak at once. Have the group decide in advance the maximum time people can talk before passing the object along to someone else.

❖ Consider appointing a different volunteer each week to enforce that time limit. It can be lighthearted—she can be the Boundary Goddess. She stops people from speaking out of turn—unless everyone has agreed in advance that there are times when others can ask to speak out of turn. But *never* are they allowed to interrupt.

❖ Occasionally allow time for participants to comment on the group process itself: Does it meet their needs? Does it help them in their development to be authentic? Does it help them with their spiritual lives?

Facilitation

Have members rotate being the facilitator. The facilitator is responsible for encouraging participation and keeping the discussion from going off on tangents. It'll take a few weeks to get a sense of the group's rhythm. Some suggestions:

❖ Unify the participants around the discovery of what the questions bring to mind. Although it's quite possible you'll all feel the same way about particular political or social issues, don't assume so. Try not to let political and social issues become the unifying factor of the group.

❖ When someone is dominating the discussion by adding comments at the end of everyone else's sharing, or continually talking too long, the facilitator can move the discussion along with one of the following:

- ▪ "How do the rest of you feel about that idea?"
- ▪ "Okay, that's a good point; now, let's hear from someone else."
- ▪ "Sara, in order to give everyone here a chance to discuss their viewpoints, I am calling time on this discussion."

If someone is continually dominating the discussion, it's most likely your job, as the go-to person, to take her aside after the meeting and talk to her. (If you feel awkward about doing this, consider that this may be a good exercise in personal growth around setting boundaries.)

You might say something like, "Sara, I noticed you talked quite a bit more tonight than anyone else, and that that's been true three weeks in a row now. [You've just stated the facts, not your opinion.] In my judgment, it's hard to give everyone a fair chance to participate when you do that. [You've just stated your judgment about the facts.] If you've got a burning issue that you really want to discuss, asking someone here to get together with you for coffee at another time would be a better idea than using the group to work through those issues. [You've just stated what you want her to do.]"

Questions for Review and Discussion

The following Reader Questions can fill meetings for ten to twelve weeks, or you can take your time and they'll easily last nine months or more. It depends on how deeply you want to engage in self-discovery and community. Perhaps you can begin with *Kick Start* and vote on other books to discuss as well.

Whatever you decide to do, I invite you to see this time as a precious respite from the mundane areas of life. Use it to practice being yourself among friends. Use it to get to know the uniqueness of each individual with love and acceptance. Most important, use it as a tool for learning more about yourself and the creative insight that invites the Real You to come out and make a difference in the world.

Introduction and Chapter 1, The SheBiker

- Identify some of the SheBikers in your life. Are there other metaphors that work for you?
- Are there women in your life who have overcome difficult situations, in terms of bucking society's mores and needing to move ahead, like the author's grandmother had to do? Have you talked to them in any depth about their experience?
- Consider sharing either the author's story or your own story with a loved one of an older generation. Discover where and when they may have undergone struggles or met with adversity.
- Do you agree with the author that as we work on expressing our authentic selves, we have a duty to help others evolve? If so, how do you think this process might begin in your life?

❖ Think about a situation in which you felt someone else was a "bitch." Now use your imagination to think of conditions that might have made her behavior understandable. How would the situation seem if you saw her in another light?

❖ Consider a time when you manipulated someone. How else might you have approached the situation? What would it have felt like to be able to say directly what you wanted and needed?

❖ How have you been shaped by retail ads? How do you approach buying your clothes and other products? Who do you look to for approval? What is your style and how did you develop it?

❖ Has there been a time in your life when you've felt you compromised your values for approval from others? Or compromised your wants or needs? How did or does this make you feel?

❖ How do you listen to your "gut"? Can you remember a time when this served you well? Are there times you listened to your gut but didn't follow it? What happened?

❖ Think about a time you supposedly failed. What did you learn about yourself from it? Are you able to have compassion for the "you" who failed? If not, why not? Are those reasons valid, or are they the voices of other people in your life?

❖ What does the "true you" look like? When you peel away all the surrounding layers you've used to protect yourself, what no longer serves you? Look at how you've evolved to date. What layers have you already peeled off? What behaviors have you already left behind? Who do you see yourself as being at the very core of your being?

CHAPTER 2, SELF-IMPOSED ROADBLOCKS

❖ List the tasks you're performing on a regular basis. Separate those you enjoy from those you don't. If your Queen SheBiker arrived at the door, which tasks would you gladly relinquish or discard?

❖ How much time do you spend on your appearance every day? For one week, take notes each day of the activities and time spent on "appearance." Are you surprised at your findings? Why or why not?

❖ What do you consider beautiful? In other people, in yourself, in the world?

❖ What does the beautiful woman inside you stand for? What does she want for the world?

❖ What values are important to you? How do you express your values in terms of how you spend your time and energy?

❖ What is the goal of your life here? If you're not clear about this, begin an internal inquiry on this topic using the process outlined in the book.

❖ How do you acknowledge and seek the spirit within that gives you a sense of value? Ask others how they accomplish this.

Chapter 3, Gearing Up for the Ride

❖ Within your family, are domestic chores shared equally? If so, do you see this as a reflection of your ability to set boundaries and assert rights for yourself in other areas? If chores are not shared equally, and you would like them to be, what is at risk if you ask for what you need in this regard?

❖ Do you know how to use truth in your communications with others? What are some of the difficulties you have when you find yourself in a difficult argument with a loved one?

❖ Do you notice any feelings or "tapes" that habitually prevent you from getting what you need at those times? Can you remember when or from whom those feelings or tapes originated in your life?

❖ Practice seeking the truth and communicating it:

1. Begin by stating the way you see the facts. Avoid blaming, judging or manipulating to skew the facts so they appear a particular way. Let them stand on their own.

2. Continue by describing how the facts of the situation make you feel and the conclusions you personally draw from those facts.

3. Complete the communication by asking for what you want.

❖ Try this three-step process without blaming the other person, but allowing your statement—of the facts, your feelings and your personal conclusions—to draw a picture of how you perceive the issue or situation. Be sure to ask for what you want rather than saying what you don't want. Be as nonmanipulative in your wording and as respectful of the other person as possible.

❖ Practice being a mirror to your loved ones so they have an arena for exploring truth. Pay careful attention to what they are saying, then repeat back to them what you heard. If it's not actually what they meant, they can explain some more. This technique will help them get clear about their thoughts and insights.

❖ Have there ever been times when you used victimhood as a crutch, allowing you to avoid responsibility or continue patterns that had nothing to do with the present moment?

❖ Have you ever been through a divorce? Describe the values you believe would have helped you deal with it more successfully.

❖ Recall a difficult episode in your past and compare the way you currently regard that episode with how it seemed at the time. Can you see how, with a more expanded perspective, the situation appears different to you? How would you have acted in that situation if you'd had an expanded perspective then?

❖ Have your friends ever abandoned you when you were in need of their support? Why do you think they did that? Have you ever, inadvertently or otherwise, abandoned your friends? What were your reasons at the time?

❖ What kind of perspective is the author using when she says we have millions of years to get it right? Do you agree with her? If not, what is your personal belief surrounding the impact of your actions on your worth as a continuing mortal in eternity?

❖ Did any feelings or judgments come up for you about the author's husband communicating with other women on the Internet?

❖ Have you ever experienced PMS? If so, does it feel correct to say that the issues you lose control over are issues you should have come clean about before they got out of hand? Or is it more of a vague anxiety or anger? Can you trace the issues or feelings to their origins?

❖ Can you feel the difference in a PMS-inspired situation and one that isn't? Try coming to an agreement with yourself in advance on how you will make your communications more effective during those times. Try using the truthful communication technique described earlier or delay your reaction until you can become more real about the issue. See how it works for you.

❖ Do you understand the difference between strength that is rebellious and strength that is creative? What are the source feelings and perspectives involved in each one?

❖ What would it require for you to get your strength from God? How would your relationship with God have to change for that to be effective for you?

❖ Do you meditate or pray on a regular basis? If not, research various meditation techniques online or by talking to others who do, and try a regular practice for a month.

❖ Are there any situations in your life in which you feel like an outsider? Why? How does it make you feel?

❖ What does the author mean about embodying a new paradigm of thinking? How would that change your identity and the way others perceive you?

❖ Reflect together on whether your group could be a better support system for you. Is there anything—besides more chocolate—that would help you embody that paradigm and be nurtured more completely in your evolving identity?

Chapter 4, Going Your Own Way

❖ The author had a life-changing experience when she was confronted with her own mortality. Have you ever experienced something similar?

❖ Think of a time when you tried to change things and were met with resistance from those around you. How did you react? What would you do differently today in terms of honoring what you were trying to accomplish?

❖ Most of us have lost friends at some time, people we once thought would always be a part of our lives. What have you learned from such experiences? What is it you feel when you think about those losses? What would you do differently today? What would you have said to those persons that you didn't get a chance to say then?

❖ What do you feel inside when you think about directing your own life? Is it a forbidden idea? Listen closely to the thoughts that come to you—can you identify who in your life originally spoke those thoughts, and when? Do you need to continue to use those thoughts for guidance, or have you outgrown them?

❖ Think of at least one person you consider to be great, someone who clearly holds a personal vision she or he follows in service to others. Identify the differences between stewardship for humanity and "knee-jerk" nurturing.

❖ Imagine what your life would be like if you committed to becoming more on the outside what you are on the inside. Instead of thinking about all the ways that would disrupt your life, think about all the ways it would improve it. In what positive ways would it affect your relationships? Your level of energy? How would it reduce your negative emotions?

❖ What sort of feelings do you experience that you can directly relate to the fact you're not living an authentic life? What positive gains do you derive from conforming to a life that is not authentic? Do you think you could have those positive things even if you didn't conform? Why or why not?

❖ Do you believe the author when she says that if you first commit to a vision, the game plan will follow? Why or why not? What has been your experience in the past?

❖ Can you recall a time in your life when you "became" what you stood for? Did you start treating people differently? Did you create new boundaries for yourself that you insisted people honor? Did you change something physically?

CHAPTER 5, ON THE ROAD TO CHANGE

❖ Is there anything in your life that is similar to the experience the author had with playing the piano?

✤ Do you live your life with the belief that enough doing will change the way you are? What are some examples?

✤ Do you ever find yourself wishing someone else in your life would be more forceful in insisting you do things that would more closely reflect who you are? Do you manipulate others until they "give you permission" to do things you secretly want to do?

✤ Describe a time when you tried to change things and, instead, your life went back to the way it had always been. What do you think happened that made the change unsuccessful?

✤ What are some issues in the world that move you, but have always appeared to be too overwhelming for you to get involved?

✤ Describe a time in your life when you used a big vision and creative tension to attain progress. What values present in the vision compelled you to take action? If you can, remember how you felt about yourself during that time.

✤ Think about your "safety ditch." What are some of the beliefs and habits you have that limit you?

✤ How do you feel about assessing your current state of reality? Do you feel anxious about it? If so, why? If not, why not?

✤ On a scale of one to ten, how authentic is the persona you present to your family? To your friends? To the general public? Why the differences?

✤ Can you recall anyone you've known or have read about who exhibited a stunning life perspective that transformed the person's situation?

✤ Do you know any other stories that describe the condition of limiting oneself in the way that *The Prison* describes?

Chapter 6, Navigating by Values

✤ In the story at the beginning of the chapter, Anna and her son's lives were being affected by one of the things Anna taught her son to avoid in his life, which was manipulating the truth to get what you want. Have you ever found yourself in a situation in which the values you believe in are being challenged by their "shadow" components?

❖ When you chose words from the list, were you surprised at the words that appealed to you? Did they confirm or reveal anything unusual?

❖ Can you give a definition of the values you stand for and offer examples of how those values play out in your life? Do you feel you have an intimate understanding of the ways in which your life is shaped by what you say you stand for?

❖ Think of someone you admire, living or not, who inspired you because they exhibited noble behavior or a higher purpose. Can you identify the values that you so admire?

❖ Do you agree with the author that love is the greatest reality? If so, can you explain your belief in that position using personal examples?

❖ The author maintains that one of the ways God loves us is by respecting our free will. Can you take that premise and expand it to satisfy your own sense of justice in the damage our free will does to this planet and to other people? If not, what questions are you left with?

❖ How has the pain you've experienced in your life made you more compassionate?

❖ Have you ever had an experience similar to that of the author's friend who went back to college to become more "qualified?" What did you learn from your experience?

❖ Think about the ways in which you identify yourself and the thoughts and beliefs that shape your life. What values are present there?

CHAPTER 7, CREATING A VISION THAT DRIVES YOU

❖ Think back over the last ten to twenty years and try to see what kinds of decisions or events led you to where you are today. Were they conscious choices, or did you simply allow the situations to dictate the outcomes?

❖ Do you take care of others in ways they could easily care for themselves? Why? What do you gain from doing that? Are those reasons important enough to take up your time, and do you get the results you're after? How else could you arrive at those results?

❖ Have you allowed the needs of others to take up more time in your life as you've grown older? Did you consciously agree to attend to those needs, or did you adopt that behavior without thinking it through?

❖ How could skills you use to take care of those around you be transformed into skills you could use to change your life into a more meaningful existence? Or will you set those caregiving skills aside as you become someone quite different?

❖ How have you felt about doing the exercises in the book? Have you been eager to answer the questions, or has it felt like a lot of work? Why?

❖ When you were writing out your answers, did you feel you needed to protect your ideas from the judgment of others? Is that feeling well founded? Why or why not?

❖ What realizations can you arrive at by reviewing your description of the life you desire? Are there any new revelations, or are all the unfulfilled aspects of your life familiar ones? What is it in your life that keeps you from actualizing these things?

❖ Think of three ways you can use your statement in your life to define the woman you are in relation to the world. What might change for you in those instances?

❖ What was it like for you to write this vision? Did you feel excited or apathetic? Did it move you or make you angry? What kinds of thoughts or judgments came up for you, and who was it in your life that originally voiced those thoughts?

❖ How do you feel about the author's declaration that your vision statement has to be inclusive of everyone? Do you think she means that you have to take care of the world? What else could she mean?

❖ What happened when you read your statement to other people? What were their reactions? If they didn't share your enthusiasm, did you feel deflated? Or did you feel that sharing your statement was still an empowering experience? Explain.

CHAPTER 8, YOUR TOOLKIT

❖ What sort of "tools" do you use to be effective in your life, such as organizational skills or a sense of humor? What other tools do you wish you had?

❖ Do you live mainly in a reactive mode or a creative mode? Think of examples of each from among your relationships and habits. Can you think of any underlying perspectives that make the difference in how you react?

❖ Think of a decision you need to make, or one you've already made. Use the list of questions from this chapter to formulate a new decision for that issue. Is it a conclusion you would have arrived at differently without the questions? If so, what was different, and does it feel better or worse? Does it make you uncomfortable? Why?

❖ Think of at least one instance when you came to the "how" of a decision before you clearly identified your goal. How did it turn out?

❖ Consider a decision or two you need to make. Make a theoretical list of what needs to be done, and check the hierarchy of decisions involved. Do you see any pattern in your decision-making process that needs to be rearranged?

❖ Think of a major decision you've made in the past, and see if the creative process described in this chapter fits your own experience.

CHAPTER 9, THE FLOW OF THE JOURNEY

❖ Do you know any stories about people who had divine mandates to carry out their mission in life? Have you ever wished you would receive divine guidance? Do you wait to make a commitment until you have some signal from the universe that it's the right thing to do?

❖ What do you think the author means when she says we would experience more conviction if we made the effort to think things through?

❖ What is your explanation of the assertion "Love is the real guide to insight"? How would love help us see things more clearly? Describe a situation in which you've experienced the truth of that assertion, as well as a situation in which love has made things less clear. Do the two situations involve the same kind of love?

❖ How has your sense of spirituality been redefined in the years since your earlier experiences with religion or spirituality?

❖ How much of your understanding of spirituality do you receive from other sources? What understanding of divine reality do you gain from your personal experience? What is the difference? Is one more real or more important than the other? Why?

❖ What is a real value? Why do you think the author cites values as a way to relate to God? Do you see values as ethical guideposts and social mores, or do you think values are more intrinsically linked to divine reality? If the latter, how do values color your experience of God?

❖ The author writes, "Trust God to take care of your soul." How do you make the distinction of who you should rely on in any given situation?

CHAPTER 10, THE ROAD AHEAD

❖ Have you seen the movie *Contact*? What do you remember of your impressions of the movie? What are your impressions of life beyond this planet? How were those impressions formed?

❖ Do you think the author could be right about having a conversation with someone from another planet in 300 years? If you knew for certain that such a conversation would take place, how would it change your perspective on what you are doing with your life right now?

❖ Do you agree with the author that there are two arenas of experience we relate to in our current lives, one being our efforts to help the planet evolve and the other being our efforts to develop ourselves? If not, why not? If so, think of at least one way in which these different efforts affect the way you make decisions.

❖ What do you think the author means by "getting really good at being who we are"? How would you develop your ability to do that?

❖ Think about the cycle the author describes of love coming from God to humans, to others, and then back to God. Do you agree with that dynamic? If so, how does that dynamic affect the way you treat others?

❖ How can you work on thinking "cosmically" instead of "globally"?

❖ Do you ever feel that others think you're being naïve when you object to the way things are? If so, does it stop you from speaking up against wrong? How might you overcome that intimidation?

❖ Did you develop a statement, outlined in chapter 5, that identifies what you stand for? If so, how will you use that statement to guide you in the future? Think of at least one way it will serve you in your everyday life.

❖ If love is the flow we tap into for power, how do you use that power in your life? How could you have a better relationship with that power to be more effective in the world and happier inside?

❖ Do you agree with the author that "you need to be playing a bigger game than you are right now"? What's holding you back?

❖ Are you registered to vote? Do you feel as much ownership in the political process as you would like to? What's stopping you from being more involved?

❖ What is your gift to the planet? What particular aspect of your experience or personality stands out for you at this moment as something that is uniquely yours to give to others?

About the Author

Carol Setters, aka the CosmicBiker, is a spiritual feminist who rides her own motorcycle. She is the founder of a community of radical women who call themselves SheBikers and "gather" at Cosmic Biker (*www.cosmicbiker.com*) to discuss ways to change the world through authentic and compassionate living. She lives in Boulder, CO. Email her at *CosmicBiker@ CosmicBiker.com* and tell her what you think.

To Our Readers

Conari Press, an imprint of Red Wheel/Weiser, publishes books on topics ranging from spirituality, personal growth, and relationships to women's issues, parenting, and social issues. Our mission is to publish quality books that will make a difference in people's lives—how we feel about ourselves and how we relate to one another. We value integrity, compassion, and receptivity, both in the books we publish and in the way we do business.

Our readers are our most important resource, and we value your input, suggestions, and ideas about what you would like to see published. Please feel free to contact us, to request our latest book catalog, or to be added to our mailing list.

Conari Press
An imprint of Red Wheel/Weiser, LLC
P.O. Box 612
York Beach, ME 03910-0612
www.conari.com